Perennial
Currents

An Imprint of HarperCollins*Publishers*

SIMPSONS COMICS BARN BURNER

FIRST EDITION

ISBN 0-06-074818-4

05 06 07 08 09 QWM 10 9 8 7 6 5 4 3 2

Publisher: MATT GROENING
Creative Director: BILL MORRISON
Managing Editor: TERRY DELEGEANE
Director of Operations: ROBERT ZAUGH
Art Director: NATHAN KANE
Art Director Special Projects: SERBAN CRISTESCU
Production Manager: CHRISTOPHER UNGAR
Legal Guardian: SUSAN A. GRODE

Trade Paperback Concepts and Design: SERBAN CRISTESCU

Contributing Artists:
KAREN BATES, TIM BAVINGTON, ART EBUEN, JASON HO, NATHAN KANE, OSCAR GONZÀLEZ LOYO,
SCOTT MCRAE, BILL MORRISON, KEVIN M. NEWMAN, PHIL ORTIZ, MIKE ROTE,
AARON ROZENFELD, CHRIS UNGAR, ART VILLANUEVA

Contributing Writers:
NEIL ALSIP, JAMES BATES, IAN BOOTHBY, DAVE MCKEAN, ERIC ROGERS,
DAVID SEIDMAN, GAIL SIMONE

PRINTED IN CANADA

TABLE OF CONTENTS

SIMPSONS COMICS #57
7   How the Vest Was Won!
27   A Swingin' Affair!

SIMPSONS COMICS #58
34   Mayor Me a Little
55   Lisa's Historical Dream

SIMPSONS COMICS #59
60   Faking the Band

SIMPSONS COMICS #60
82   The Man with Two Wives
104 My Sister, My Sidekick!

SIMPSONS COMICS #61
111 The Paper Chase

SIMPSONS COMICS #63
134 The Bogey Man
155 Groundskeeper Willie's History of Golf
156 ...If Homer Simpson Invented Golf!

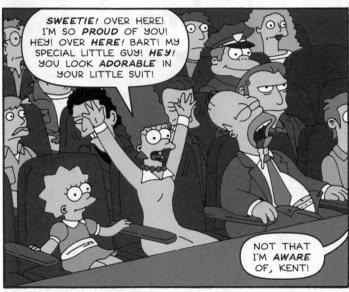

"UH...MAYBE YOU SHOULD SKIP *PAST* THIS PART, KENT."

SCRUB ME TWO TIMES, ONE FOR TOMORROW, ONE FOR JUST TODAY–DA, DA, DA, DA, SCRUB ME TWO TIMES... I'M GOING AWAY!

"KEEP *GOIN'*..."

To my #1 fan, "LISA," Corey

"HERE WE GO! I WAS...UH...CONTINUING MY *"RESEARCH,"* WHEN I NOTICED AN UNSAVORY *GANG OF YOUTHS* ENTERING THE *KWIK-E-MART*..."

BARELY SENILE

Sensous Single Moms

Hemp Made HOT RODS

INSIDE! THE GIRLS OF MEALS ON WHEELS!

ADULTS ONLY

"MY FINELY-TUNED SENSES DETECTED THAT *TROUBLE* WAS A'BREWIN'!"

"SEE KENT, PART OF THE *"POSSE"* DISTRACTED THE *CLERK*, WHILE THE *REAL* MASTERMIND MADE A *DASH* FOR THE *STOCKROOM!*"

MAKE WAY, *WIMP*SON!

"HERE WE SEE ONE OF THE *"PERPS"* ESCAPING WITH HIS *ILL-GOTTEN GOODS!*"

LABIOS CALIENTES

...AND THEN I CALLED *1-800-I SQUEAL* AND THE REST IS LAW-ENFORCEMENT *HISTORY*, KENT!

WELL *DONE*, YOUNG CRIMESTOPPER! WE NOW CONTINUE THE STORY WITH SPRINGFIELD'S TOP COP, *POLICE CHIEF CLANCY WIGGUM!*

CLAP! CLAP! CLAP!

WELL, KENT, BASED ON THE EVIDENCE PRESENTED BY YOUNG BART SIMPSON, WE APPREHENDED THE *ENTIRE GANG* THAT SAME EVENING. A POLICE FORCE LIKE OURS IS ONLY AS GOOD AS ITS *DIRTY SNITCHES*.

WAP! WAP! WAP!

SO, WHAT *WAS* IN THE CRATE THAT THE YOUNG HOODLUMS STOLE? HARD LIQUOR? LOTTERY TICKETS? THOSE NEW FOOD STAMPS COMMEMORATING THE 60'S?

EH...AHEH, NO, KENT! IT TURNS OUT THAT WHAT THEY *THOUGHT* WAS A CASE OF *MEXICAN BEER* WAS IN FACT A CASE OF *WAX LIPS!* AHEH-HEH!

HA HA HA HA HA HA!

MY DADDY LETS ME PLAY IN THE *EVIDENCE LOCKER!*

WELL, *THIS* REPORTER FOR ONE IS GLAD TO HEAR THAT THESE *VICIOUS YOUNG PUNKS* ARE LOCKED UP *GOOD AND TIGHT*, WHERE THEY CAN'T SEEK *BLOOD-THIRSTY REVENGE* ON OUR UPSTANDING YOUNG CITIZEN, HERE.

AH...YOU'D *THINK* THAT, WOULDN'T YOU? AS IT TURNS OUT, THE JUDGE LET THEM OFF WITH AN *HOUR* OF *COMMUNITY SERVICE*. BUT DON'T YOU *WORRY*! AT LEAST DURING TONIGHT'S *BROADCAST*, I'VE GOT THEM *RIGHT* WHERE I *WANT* THEM!

BART SIMPSON, FOR YOUR *BRAVERY* IN THE FACE OF POSSIBLE *VIOLENT RETRIBUTION*, WE AWARD YOU THIS *"LI'L SQUEALER"* BULLET-PROOF VEST.

THE SAME TYPE WORN BY *MANY* STILL-LIVING LAW ENFORCEMENT OFFICERS AND WHACKED-OUT CONSPIRACY THEORISTS!

COOL, MAN!

⦂CHUCKLE⦂ ...AND FROM THE LOOKS OF THOSE *VENGEFUL YOUNG THUGS*, YOU'LL *NEED* IT!

HAHAHAHA

WE'LL *GET* YOU FOR THIS, SIMPSON! YOU'LL *CURSE* THE DAY YOU DECIDED TO LIVE BY *SOCIETY'S LAWS*!

DOWN IN FRONT!

SOON...

KLOP
KLOP KLOP
KLOP

...PRINCE, MARTIN...

HERE!

SIMPSON, BART... *BART?*...NO?

STUDENT LIST
PRINCE, M.
SIMPSON, B.

HA! IT'S MY *LUCKY DAY!*

STUDENT LIST
PRINCE, M.
SIMPSON, B.

WHAAM!

NOT SO *FAST,* MRS. KRABAPPEL!

ME *AND MY VEST* ARE *PRESENT* AND *ACCOUNTED FOR,* MA'AM!

HE LOOKS LIKE A *MOVIE STAR!*

BEHOLD THE POWER THAT IS *BART!*

WOW!

¡KAFF!¿

ACTUALLY, IT SHOULD BE "MY VEST AND *I*," BUT SINCE I CAN SEE NO ACTUAL *LEARNING* WILL TAKE PLACE TODAY, WHO CARES? TAKE YOUR SEAT, BART.

YOU *GOT* IT, BABE!

YOU *SNITCHED* ON ME, *SIMPSON,* AND YOU'RE GONNA *PAY,* VEST BOY. IT AIN'T GONNA BE JUST WEDGIES AND DUTCH RUBS *THIS* TIME!

ULP!

LATER, AT RECESS...

...RUNNING WITH SCISSORS? OH YEAH, I COULD RUN WITH SCISSORS *ALL DAY LONG,* IF I WANTED TO. AND LAWN DARTS? WELL, LET'S JUST SAY...*NO PROBLEMO!*

OOOOH!

MY *DADDY* SAYS ROBOTS ARE *EVIL!*

I'D LIKE TO *REMIND* EVERYONE HERE THAT BART'S VEST IS MERELY A BULLET-*RESISTANT* GARMENT AND DOES NOT IN FACT MAKE HIM A *ROBOT* OR *SUPERHERO.*

UH, HUH. AND I SUPPOSE YOUR *POCKET PROTECTOR* IS GOING TO SAVE YOU WHEN THE *ALIENS* START *BLASTING?*

OOOOOH!!

BART WILL *PROTECT* US FROM *THE FIRE IN THE SKY!*

WHO SAYS THE YOUTH OF TODAY AREN'T GOAL-ORIENTED?!

ALL RIGHT, WE'RE ALL *AGREED*. IT'S A *BLOOD PACT*. RIGHT AFTER WE DO OUR *COMMUNITY SERVICE* TONIGHT, WE DEVOTE OUR *ENTIRE LIVES* TO DESTROYING BART SIMPSON! NO ONE WIMPS OUT UNTIL HE'S *HISTORY*!

WE'RE CROSSING THE LINE HERE, DUDES, FROM MISDEMEANOR TO FELONY! SIMPSON'S GOT TO BE *DEALT* WITH *SEVERELY*!

SO SAY WE ALL!

MAN, I NEVER THOUGHT I'D *SAY* THIS, BUT I AM *SO SICK* OF SPIT-CLEANING THIS DUDE'S *BUTT*!

I DON'T FEEL *EMBIGGENED* AT ALL!

MR. SPARKLE
PIGEON CRAP
FORMULA
For Unsightly
Stains and
Hip Jeans!

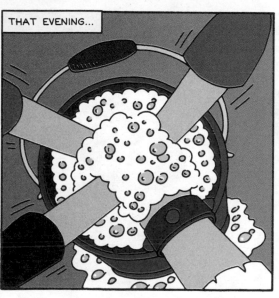

THAT EVENING...

THE NEXT MORNING...

♪ WHEN I'M WASHIN' IN MY *WILD, WILD VEST!* AND I'M RINSIN' IN MY *WILD WILD VEST!* WHOO! HA! ♪ *WILD, WILD VEST!*

BART! HURRY OR YOU'LL BE LATE!

OH, YEAH, MOM. LATE FOR *SCHOOL.* THAT *WOULD* BE A TRAGEDY.

NOW LOOK, BART...

MOM, I *KNOW* YOU'RE GOING TO GIVE ME A *LECTURE* ABOUT WEARING MY *VEST* TO *SCHOOL.* BUT HOW ABOUT WE BOTH JUST *ADMIT* THAT THE VEST IS *WAY* TOO COOL TO EVER TAKE OFF AND I'LL BE ON MY WAY?

FOR YOUR *INFORMATION,* YOUNG MAN, I WAS JUST GOING TO *INFORM* YOU THAT YOU FORGOT YOUR *PANTS.*

AYE CARUMBA!

SHORTLY...

HI, BART! I FIGURED I'D WAIT HERE FOR YOU IN CASE YOU NEEDED HELP CARRYING YOUR *BOOKS* OR SOMETHING!

WELL, OKAY, BUT JUST UNTIL SOMEONE *BETTER* ASKS TO DO IT.

I WOULDN'T HAVE IT *ANY OTHER WAY!*

...AND SO, THE GAME *BEGINS.* *SIMPSON,* YOUR TIME IS AT HAND!

HEY! THEY GOT *TEAR GAS* IN HERE! AND *DONUTS!* AND *SURVEILLANCE PHOTOS* OF MY *SISTER!* EEW, *DUDE!*

17

AFTER SCHOOL...

ALL QUIET HERE, *BART!* NO SIGN OF NELSON'S GANG! YOU'RE CLEAR TO GO *HOME!*

HEY! ALL MY PARENTS' *WEDDING PICTURES* ARE IN HERE!

STAY *FOCUSED,* MILHOUSE! THESE GUYS WANT ME *DEAD!* JUST STAY THERE IN THE *OBSERVATION BUNKER* AND KEEP AN *EYE* OUT!

UH...BY "*OBSERVATION BUNKER,*" YOU MEAN THE *DUMPSTER,* RIGHT?

YEP.

HEY, I THINK SOMETHING JUST SLITHERED INTO MY SHOE! I'M GETTING OUT FOR A SECOND SO I CAN CHECK IT... *KRAAAASH!*

BARRK BARRK

SNARRL SNAP

BARK!

GRRRRRRRRRRRRRR!

NOW!!!

HA! EAT *CANINE,* SIMPSON!

20

MILHOUSE! AS A KISS-UP, YOU'RE A COMPLETE *FAILURE!* THOSE GUYS ALMOST *GOT* ME! WHERE WERE *YOU* WITH THE *DANGER ALERT?*

IT'S NOT MY *FAULT,* BART!

I STEPPED OUT TO CHECK MY SHOE, AND A CHUNK OF THE OLD *MONORAIL TRACK* DESTROYED THE *OBSERVATION BUNKER!*

OH, MY DUMPSTER! THAT IS THE THIRD TIME THIS WEEK! WHERE ARE MY WINO CUSTOMERS SUPPOSED TO SLEEP?

AH, I SEE THAT YOU ARE WEARING THE *DOMINATOR MARK IV MODEL PERSONAL ARMORED VEST!* GOOD STOPPING POWER, AND IT LOOKS SO SNAPPY, TOO!

WHY, IT IS AS MUCH AT HOME ON THE DANCE FLOOR AS IT IS DURING A HOSTAGE CRISIS!

MEANWHILE...

...AND NOW IT'S DOWN TO JUST BART AND THE TWO OF US. I SEE WHERE WE MADE OUR *MISTAKE.* WE TRIED TO UNLEASH THE *AWESOME FURY OF NATURE* ON SIMPSON, AND WE PAID *DEARLY* FOR IT. TIME FOR A NEW PLAN.

POLICE

AW, LET'S JUST BEAT THE *CRUD* OUT OF HIM.

THERE HE IS! MAN, I *KNEW* THIS DRIVING AROUND POINTLESSLY WOULD *PAY OFF!*

RUN HIM DOWN!

AAAAAAAH!

THIS WAY! I KNOW A SHORTCUT *HOME!*

YOU'RE *DEAD*, SIMPSON! MIGHT AS WELL *GIVE UP* SO WE DON'T GET *TOO TIRED* TO BEAT *YOU!*

6411

SPRINGFIE TIRE YAR

COMBUSTIBLES WELCOME!

...RETREAD DAY...HERE AT...THE *SPRINGFIELD TIRE YARD*...HOME OF THE...NEVER-ENDING *TIRE FIRE*.

WE DON'T BURN TIRES IN YOUR TOILET, PLEASE DON'T PEE IN OUR DUMP!

SIGH *TEN YEARS* AS A REPORTER ON THIS BEAT AND I *STILL* GET STUCK WITH THE *TIRE YARD REPORT*. I NEVER THOUGHT I'D SAY THIS, BUT I'M *SICK* OF THE SMELL OF *BURNING TIRES*.

ALL RIGHT, HOW LONG HAVE YOU WORKED HERE, BUDDY?

AW, NO! I DON'T WORK HERE *ATALL*, MISTER! MIND YEW, I *HOPES* TO WORK HERE SOME-A-DAY.

RIGHT NOW, I JEST COMES HERE FER THE *GRANDEUR* AND THE *SPECTACLE*.

WE DON'T URN TIRES IN YOUR OILET, PLEASE DON'T EE IN OUR DUMP!

Springfield Shopper

Weather: Acid Rain
Stock Market:
The cupboard is BEAR!

Where News Isn't Just About The Facts

Today's Winning
Lotto Numbers:
4-13-21-4-35

HEROIC LOCAL BOY BERT STIMPSON SAVES PLAYMATE WILSON MUMPS!

by Dave Shutton

There are two things that the Springfield Tire Yard has in abundance; low, low prices and over an acre of burning tires. Today, they have something else in great supply—Heroism.

Springfield's most recent recipient of the coveted "Li'l Squealer" award, Bert Stimpson, again showed his true colors when he saved school buddy Wilson Mumps from a falling piece of the decaying monorail track. Neither Bert nor Wilson suffered serious injury, due to both Bert's quick thinking, and his convenient body armor, won on this week's "Kids Commit the Darndest Crimes" program.

This reporter hasn't got a friend in the world who would throw themselves in the way of a huge piece of concrete. It causes me to reflect on how pathetic my life has become and (continued on page 4a)

(continued on page 4a)

Local weiner,
Dilhouse Von Hootin

HERO'S "BEST FRIEND" IS A COWARD!

by Dave Shutton

And what was Bert's best friend Dilhouse doing when all this heroism was taking place?

"I was afraid and I ran. They made me eat my pencil case once," said the whiny little yellow-belly. "Hey! Quit calling me names! I'm telling!" continued the sniveling little cry-baby (continued on page 4a)

Young Bert Stimpson proudly holds his new axe, which he has nicknamed "Choppy."

HERO BOY RECEIVES SECOND AWARD

by Dave Shutton

It isn't often a ten year-old boy receives the admiration and gratitude of an entire community, and it's even more rare for that same boy to be so honored twice in the same week.

When asked about the special gift given to him during the ceremony put on by the Springfield Volunteer Fire Department, young Bert Stimpson remarked, "Oh, yeah, this baby will come in real handy!"

So, will the young man still need his former award, a bullet-proof vest? "Not now that I have this shiny new ax for protection, man!"

LOCAL P.E.T.A. CHAPTER RESCUES POSSUM

"He had a cheese puff lodged in his windpipe," says local P.E.T.A. volunteer Bernie Gimple. "I had to give him mouth-to-mouth. He bit me real bad. Real bad! OWWWWW!" (story continued on page 5a)

WILL THE MONORAIL TRACK HIT YOUR HOME?

We don't want to alarm you, but short answer? Yes.
(story continued on page 5a)

TEN MINUTES 'TIL DINNER, MY *SPECIAL LITTLE HERO GUY!*

WHACK!

YEP. IT FEELS *MIGHTY FINE* TO BE A HERO, ESPECIALLY A HERO WITH A PINE-HANDLED WOOD-SLICIN', RAZOR-SHARP, OFFICIAL *FIREMAN'S AX,* BABY!

NELSON!

HEY, SIMPSON. I JUST WANTED TO LET YOU KNOW: YOU COST ME AN HOUR OF *STATUE-POLISHIN',* AND THEN YOU *SAVED MY LIFE.* I FIGURE THAT MAKES US ABOUT *EVEN.*

IT'S NOT A *GOOD* DEAL, BUT I'LL *TAKE* IT!

NICE *AX,* SIMPSON. IT'S GOT REAL VANDALISM POTENTIAL. SO, NOT WEARING YOUR *VEST* ANYMORE?

NAH. THOSE STRAPS WERE REALLY STARTING TO *RIDE UP.*

"BESIDES, I REALIZED YOU HAVE TO BE A REAL DORK TO WALK AROUND WEARING A BULLETPROOF VEST!"

DON'T LOOK UP—IT'S *THE END!*

...AND ON THE LIGHTER SIDE, IT APPEARS THAT THE RUMORS OF THE *DEATH OF SWING* HAVE BEEN GREATLY EXAGGERATED! IT'S ALIVE AND WELL IN SPRINGFIELD!

THE *WHOLE TOWN'S* BOPPIN' TO THOSE CRAZY RIFFS OF THE 30'S AND 40'S AND JOINTS FROM *SHOTKICKERS* TO *BLOATERS AT THE SQUIDPORT* ARE GETTIN' *HEP TO IT!*

HOMER, THAT SOUNDS LIKE A GOOD TIME! LET'S GO *DANCING!*

BUT MARGE, THAT STUFF'S *DANGEROUS!*

DON'T YOU KNOW HOW MANY PEOPLE *DIE* FROM DANCE-FLOOR SPLINTERS? THEY DON'T STERILIZE THE TWEEZERS AT THOSE PLACES!

WELL, THAT TOO...

YOU DON'T WANT TO SWING BECAUSE IT'S *STRENUOUS*. YOU'RE JUST LAZY AND SLUGGISH.

A Swingin' Affair!

DAVID SEIDMAN
STORY

OSCAR GONZÁLEZ LOYO
PENCILS

SCOTT MCRAE
INKS

CHRIS UNGAR
COLORS

KAREN BATES
LETTERS

BILL MORRISON
EDITOR

MATT GROENING
THE BEES KNEES

...BUT ISN'T SLUGGISHNESS A LITTLE...*SEXY?*

NO! I'M GOING DANCING, AND IF *YOU* WON'T TAKE ME, I'LL FIND SOMEONE WHO *WILL!*

LATER...

I DON'T KNOW WHAT TO *DO,* MAUDE. MOST MEN I KNOW ARE *MARRIED,* AND THEIR WIVES DON'T WANT ME GOING OUT WITH THEIR HUSBANDS. WELL, EXCEPT THE WIFE OF THE ONE EVERYONE CALLS JIMMY THE SCUMBAG.

WHAT ABOUT THE *UNMARRIED* ONES?

I DIDN'T ASK.

DON'T MEAN TO SHATTER YOUR CHATTER, MARGE, BUT I'D BE *HAPPY* TO WHIP YOU 'ROUND THE FLOOR. WHY, IN MY *SUNDAY-SCHOOL* DAYS, I TOOK THE BRONZE IN OUR HOKEY-POKEYATHLON.

MAUDE, IS IT O.K. WITH *YOU?*

WHATEVER NED WANTS IS FINE WITH ME. OF COURSE, WE'VE ALREADY *PLANNED* TO STAY IN AND READ BIBLE STORIES. WE'RE UP TO THE GENERATIONS OF ESAU, INCLUDING THE SONS OF OHOLIBAMAH, GRANDDAUGHTER OF ZIBEON.

THEN IT'S *SETTLED!*

TONIGHT, MARGE, YOU AND I DO THE *SWING* THING!

SUDDENLY, I'VE GOT SECOND THOUGHTS, BUT ...OKAY.

...AND IF YOU HEAR ANYTHING FROM BART'S ROOM, THE NUMBERS FOR THE BOMB SQUAD AND THE HAZMAT TEAM ARE BY THE PHONE.

THAT'S IT! I'LL SEE YOU LATER.

BUT WHAT'LL I DO WHILE YOU'RE GONE?

WHAT YOU *ALWAYS* DO: DRINK BEER AND WATCH TV.

OKAY. SEE YOU!

SLAM!

WELL, BACK TO TV--WONDERFUL, WONDERFUL TV. MARGE, CAN YOU BRING ME A BEER?

OH. RIGHT.

WELL, FINE. I DON'T NEED MARGE. I CAN BE HAPPY ALL ALONE WITH MY THOUGHTS.

UH, OH.

MAUDE, WOULDJA MIND TAKING CARE OF MY KIDS FOR A FEW HOURS?

WELL, YES, HOMER, I WOULD.

YES, HUH? WELL, HERE THEY ARE! MAGGIE JUST FILLED HER DIAPER. 'BYE!

SO MARGE THINKS SHE CAN LEAVE ME AT HOME WHILE SHE GOES OUT. WELL, I CAN GO OUT ON *MY* OWN--TO GOOD OL' *MOE'S TAVERN*, WHERE I CAN DRINK MYSELF BLIND WITH DERELICTS WHO I HUG LIKE BROTHERS WHEN I'M DRUNK AND WON'T EVEN KNOW WHEN I'M SOBER.

AND THERE IT IS NOW...

D'OH!

Moe's Swingatorium

IT DON'T MEAN A THING IF YOU AIN'T GOT THAT $4.50 COVER CHARGE.

OII, NO...

...I WANT TO GIVE YOU AS GOOD A TIME AS STUPID FLANDERS. BUT I CAN'T DO IT, SO IF YOU WANT TO LEAVE ME AND LIVE WITH FLANDERS, YOU CAN, AS LONG AS YOU LIVE CLOSE ENOUGH SO I CAN KEEP TRYING TO WIN YOU BACK AND BRING YOU MY LAUNDRY SO YOU CAN STARCH MY SHIRTS THE WAY I LIKE THEM.

MMMM... STARCH....

I MEAN--MARGE, I LOVE YOU!

AND I LOVE YOU, HOMEY. I JUST WANTED YOU TO COME OUT AND DANCE WITH ME.

THEN I WILL! PLAY THAT FUNKY MUSIC, WHITE PEOPLE!

WITH WHAT?

UH, OH!

SEE, I TOLD YOU, MARGE!...

...DANCING'S DANGEROUS!

THE END

32

Mayor me a little

IF I'M ELECTED, I PROMISE A **COLD ONE** IN EVERY MUG!

JAMES BATES
STORY

OSCAR GONZÁLEZ LOYO
PENCILS

TIM BAVINGTON
INKS

ART VILLANUEVA
COLORS

KAREN BATES
LETTERS

BILL MORRISON
EDITOR

MATT GROENING
LAME DUCK

ONE EVENING, AT 742 EVERGREEN TERRACE...

C'MON, BART, TURN THE CHANNEL! I'M GOING TO BE ON THE NEWS!

NO WAY, MAN. THIS IS MY *FAVORITE* RE-RUN OF "KNIGHT BOAT."

KNIGHT BOAT IS FIGHTING THE *EVIL MONKEYS* DRIVING JET SKIS!

IT WILL BE NICE TO SEE A SIMPSON ON TV ONCE WHERE *PUBLIC DRUNKENNESS* OR THE IRE OF THE FIRE DEPARTMENT ARE NOT INVOLVED

CLICK!

HERE IT IS. WE DIDN'T MISS IT.

YOU'VE HEARD OF PEKING DUCK. WELL IN SPRINGFIELD TODAY THE *HOT ISSUE* IS OVER *PARKING* DUCK.

SPRINGFIELD DUCK PONDTROVERSY

"ONE OF SPRINGFIELD'S LAST REMAINING *UNDISTURBED* NATURE SPOTS–*THE OLD DUCK POND*, IS IN *DANGER* OF BECOMING..."

"...JUST ANOTHER PARKING STRUCTURE. NOT EVERYONE IS WILLING TO STAND IDLY BY AND LET THIS HAPPEN. WE SPOKE TO ONE PROTESTOR..."

DOWN WITH PARKING!

UP WITH DOWN!

PARKING = DEATH

DUCKS ARE PEOPLE TOO

NEED DOOBIE BROS. TIX

SAVE THE DUCKS!

DON'T BE DA SAVE OUR DUCKS

"...LISA SIMPSON."

THANK YOU FOR LETTING US BE *HEARD!* WE FEEL THAT THIS LITTLE POND WITH ITS DUCKS *SYMBOLIZES* ALL OF *NATURE.* IT WAS *HENRY DAVID THOREAU* WHO SAID, "NATURE IS FULL OF GENIUS, FULL OF DIVINITY; SO THAT A...

WE INTERRUPT THE *TRIVIAL* DUCK POND STORY TO REPORT YET *ANOTHER SCANDAL* INVOLVING MAYOR QUIMBY! APPARENTLY, WHILE SERVING AS A JUDGE AT THE *MISS SPRINGFIELD PAGEANT,* HE OFFERED A *CONTESTANT* A QUICK WAY TO GET A COUPLE *"LEGS UP"* ON THE *COMPETITION.*

HANKY PANKY GATE VII

THIS LATEST *INFIDELITY* COULDN'T COME AT A *WORSE* TIME FOR QUIMBY, WHOSE *FAVORABILITY RATING* HAS DIPPED SO *LOW* THAT HE IS IN DANGER OF *LOSING* THE *UPCOMING ELECTION,* EVEN THOUGH HE RUNS *UNOPPOSED!*

I'M *RUINED.*

CLICK!

YOU HAVE TO *HELP* ME!

DO I?

EH, I MEAN, CAN'T WE *WORK SOMETHING OUT?*

I'LL MAKE YOU AN *OFFER* YOU CAN'T *REFUSE.*

...AND SO WE UNDERSTAND THE *GREAT VIRTUES* OF *FORGIVING.* IN THE SPIRIT OF TODAY'S SERMON— *WHO* IS BRIMMING WITH FORGIVENESS?

I DIDDILY AM!

DOWN IN FRONT!

LET'S ALL JOIN NED AND WELCOME *MAYOR QUIMBY!*

37

ER, UH, HELLO.

GRRR...

LOUSY SONUVA...

NO GOOD, ROTTEN...

WHY I OUGHTTA...

DO SOMETHING! THEY LOOK *FURIOUS*, LIKE THEY JUST LEFT A TRAVOLTA MOVIE!

PEACE

FORGIVENESS, PEOPLE. TODAY'S SERMON WAS ABOUT *FORGIVENESS*! MAYOR QUIMBY HAS COME HERE TO *REPENT* AND TO PROVE HIS *SINCERITY*, HE HAS AN *ANNOUNCEMENT*!

UNDER THE ADVISEMENT OF REVEREND LOVEJOY, I'M IMPOSING *SUNDAY BLUE LAWS* TO SAVE THE *MORALS* OF SPRINGFIELD!

≡MUMBLE- MUMBLE≡

THAT'S A *GREAT* IDEA!

I MUST ADMIT THAT IDEA'S A *DANDY!*

WOO-HOO! BLUE LAWS *RULE!* *BLUE SUCKS! BAN BLUE!*

YOU'RE A *GENIUS.*

I HAVE MY MOMENTS.

HOMER, DO YOU KNOW WHAT SUNDAY BLUE LAWS *MEAN?*

OF COURSE I DO. DO YOU THINK I'M SOME KIND OF AN *IDIOT?*

CAN I ANSWER THAT?

I'M SURPRISED YOU'D SUPPORT ANY LAW THAT *BANS DRINKING BEER.*

HUH?

BANS DRINKING...

;GASP!;

NO BEER?!!

YOU *MONSTER!* HOW *DARE* YOU?

AS LONG AS I'M MAYOR, THERE'LL BE *NO BEER* ON, ER, SUNDAYS.

WELL THEN YOU *CAN'T* BE MAYOR ANY MORE. IT'S TIME YOU'RE *VOTED OUT OF OFFICE!*

I'VE BEEN RE-ELECTED *FIVE* TIMES. WHO'S GONNA BEAT ME? *YOU?*

MOE'S

SIMPSON FOR MAYOR

KEG PARTY HEADQUARTERS

Duff!

IT'S A *BEAUTIFUL THING* YOU'RE DOING THERE, HOMER.

WHEN INJUSTICE REARS ITS UGLY HEAD, AND THE DEMOCRATS AND REPUBLICANS FAIL AMERICA, WE CAN ALWAYS TURN TO THE *KEG PARTY!*

THE KEG PARTY!

CLINK!

I'M DONE MAKIN' THE SIGNS.

SIMPSON HEEL DO WUTZ RITE!

HOMER 4 MARE

Duff!

SIMPSON HEEL DO WUTZ RITE!

HOMER 4 MARE

NICE WORK, BOY.

EXCUSE ME...

WOW.

EEK!

IT'S FAT TONY!

THE MOBSTER!

WHERE IS THIS *HOMER J. SIMPSON* WHO WANTS TO BE MAYOR?

PLEASE DON'T *KILL* ME.

YOU MISUNDERSTAND ME, MR. SIMPSON. I AM HERE TO OFFER MY, UH, *UNIQUE SUPPORT*.

I THINK YOU MIGHT NEED TO RUN A SLIGHTLY MORE *UPSCALE* CAMPAIGN WITH *ME* AS YOUR *CAMPAIGN MANAGER*.

SORRY. *MOE* IS MY CAMPAIGN MANAGER.

EVEN THE *PLAYDUDE* CHANNEL?

I CAN MAKE IT WORTH YOUR WHILE. HOW ABOUT *FREE CABLE*? THE *EXTENDED* PACKAGE.

OF COURSE.

MOE, POUR MY *NEW* CAMPAIGN MANAGER A BEER!

The Springfield Shopper

DAILY NEWS   FREE

SIMPSON CAMPAIGN IN FULL SWING

EDUCATION WILL BE A PRIORITY TO MY ADMINISTRATION. I GUARAN- TEE A *NEW* AND *BETTER* CONTRACT FOR THE TEACHERS' UNION!

IMPROVED CARE FOR SENIORS IS AT THE *CENTER* OF THE SIMPSON CAMPAIGN.

MMM... OLD PEOPLE JELL-O.

NEW STADIUM? *NO PROBLEM!*

AT FIRST I THOUGHT THIS WAS ALL ABOUT *BEER* BUT YOU REALLY SEEM TO WANT TO *HELP* PEOPLE. I'M SO *PROUD* OF YOU, DAD.

THANKS, HONEY.

I KNOW YOU'VE BEEN MAKING A LOT OF OTHER *PROMISES* BUT...

WHAT IS IT, LISA?

WOULD YOU *SAVE THE DUCK POND*!

SURE! *I PROMISE*!

ISOTOPES SCHEDULE

BOSS, I'VE GOT SOME NEWS...

DAD, YOU'RE THE *GREATEST*.

The Springfield Shopper

FREE

DAILY NEWS

UPSTART CANDIDATE SIMPSON UP IN POLLS

QUIMBY SEEKS AUDIENCE WITH THE POPE

The Springfield Shopper

DAILY NEWS

TEACHERS, ATHLETES AND BREWERIES ENDORSE CHALLENGER

GLEE CLUB SUPPORTS MAYOR

The Springfield Shopper

FREE

DAILY NEWS

REVEREND CLAIMS SIMPSON HAS MADE DEAL WITH DEVIL

CANDIDATES TO HOLD RALLIES AS ELECTION DAY APPROACHES

AT A RALLY FOR MAYOR QUIMBY...

...AND REMEMBER THAT ALTHOUGH THE BIBLE TELLS US THAT JESUS TURNED WATER INTO WINE, IT SAYS NOTHING ABOUT EVIL, EVIL BEER!

QUIMBY FOR MAYOR

First Church Springfield

REFRESHMENTS ARE AVAILABLE IN THE CHURCH BASEMENT. PLEASE REMEMBER TO ENJOY THE BUTTER COOKIES IN *MODERATION*.

MEANWHILE, AT THE DUCK POND...

SIMPSON FOR MAYOR RALLY PRESENTED BY DUFF BEER

SIMPSON FOR MAYOR

SIMPSON FOR MAYOR

SUNDAY, SUDSIE SUNDAY! —NO BLUE LAWS!

SAVE THE DUCKS!

LET'S HEAR IT FOR *THE SEVEN DUFFS!*

NOW, I'D LIKE TO INTRODUCE SPRINGFIELD'S MOST *INFLUENTIAL* BUSINESS LEADER WHO HAS AN *IMPORTANT MESSAGE* FOR YOU. *FAT TONY D'AMICO!*

CLAP! CLAP! CLAP! CLAP!

VOTE FOR HOMER--

--OR ELSE.

CLAP! CLAP! CLAP!

BACK AT THE QUIMBY RALLY...

WHAT A STIRRING RENDITION OF "MICHAEL ROW THE BOAT ASHORE." LET'S, AH, HEAR IT AGAIN FOR THE, ER, AH, *SPRINGFIELD SILVER FOXES LADIES' CHOIR!*

WOO HOO! YOU'RE THE BEE'S KNEES!

ENCORE! ENCORE!

CONSARNIT! CAN'T GET THESE *BLOOMERS* OFF SO I CAN THROW 'EM AT THE CHOIR.

AND NOW, I'LL SHOW YOU *PRIDE, LUST, GREED, SLOTH, ENVY, AVARICE,* AND, OF COURSE, *GLUTTONY* IN ONE UGLY BUNDLE. I'LL SHOW YOU--

HOMER SIMPSON!

I'M SCARED! WHAT SHOULD WE *DO?*

I THINK WE'RE SUPPOSED TO *SLING MUD!*

MEANWHILE...

SPLASH!

LOOK WHAT YOU'VE *DONE!*

I CAN'T LOOK. HANGOVER...TOO STRONG. SUN BAD, DARK GOOD.

SERVES YOU RIGHT.

HE SAID IT'D BE FREE BECAUSE HE *OWNS* THE LAND.

IT JUST MAKES NO SENSE. WHY WOULD FAT TONY HAVE YOU HOLD THE RALLY *HERE?*

Lisa: OF COURSE! IT'S *HIS* PARKING STRUCTURE PLAN! HE'S USING YOU AND THE BLUE LAW *CONTROVERSY* TO *DIVERT ATTENTION* AWAY FROM THE DUCK POND!

Homer: HE SAID THAT HE'D GET ME ELECTED AS LONG AS I AGREED TO DO *EVERYTHING* HE SAYS ONCE I'M IN OFFICE. IT'S WHAT WE ADULTS CALL *POL-I-TICS.*

Lisa: YOU CAN'T LET HIM GET AWAY WITH THIS!

Homer: BUT HONEY, I'M GONNA WIN. DON'T YOU WANT ME TO BE MAYOR? WOULDN'T THAT MAKE YOU *PROUD?*

Lisa: I *WAS* PROUD OF YOU. NOW I CAN'T EVEN STAND TO *LOOK* AT YOU.

Homer: I'LL *SHOW* YOU, LISA.

SIMPSON HEEL EL DO WUTZ RITE

LEGITIMATE BUSINESSMAN'S SOCIAL CLUB

Homer: FAT TONY, YOU'VE BEEN *USING ME!* I CAN SEE THAT NOW, AND I'M HERE TO TELL YOU I DON'T *WANT* YOUR HELP *ANY MORE.* MAYOR HOMER J. SIMPSON WON'T BE ANYONE'S *PUPPET!*

Fat Tony: I SEE, AND I RESPECT YOUR DESIRE FOR *INDEPENDENCE.*

Homer: YOU DO?

Fat Tony: YES, I DO. NOW PLEASE GO WITH LEGS AND LOUIE. THEY ARE GOING TO TAKE YOU FOR A RIDE TO THE *DESERT.*

LATER...

...AND I WAS STUPID TO LET THE BAD MEN *USE* ME, BUT I WANT TO WIN.

SO YOU CAN DRINK ON SUNDAYS?

NO, SO THAT WE CAN *SAVE THE DUCKS* AND MAYBE MY DAUGHTER MIGHT *FORGIVE* ME.

OH, DAD!

DOES THIS MEAN YOU FORGIVE *ME*? AND YOU'LL BE MY *NEW* CAMPAIGN MANGER?

UH, HUH!

NEXT MORNING...

The Springfield Shopper

FREE

DAILY NEWS

DOWN TO THE WIRE!

CHALLENGER STILL CAMPAIGNING ON ELECTION DAY!

THAT'S ONE *UGLY* BABY.

SHHH!

NAME'S SIMPSON, AND I'M FOR THE *WORKIN' MAN.*

HOMER? IT'S ME, YOUR *GOOD FRIEND, LENNY!*

GOOD TO MEET YA, LARRY. I'D APPRECIATE YOUR HELP AT THE POLLS.

PLEASE HAVE A "SIMPSON FOR MAYOR" PAMPHLET. IT'S PRINTED ON *BIO-DEGRADABLE RECYCLED PAPER* AND DETAILS OUR *PRO-ENVIRONMENT AGENDA!*

LATER, THAT NIGHT...

MOE'S

AND THE *FINAL RESULTS* ARE IN...

WE HAVE A *TIE!* WHAT AN AMAZING TURN OF EVENTS! I GUESS IT'S TRUE THAT *EVERY VOTE COUNTS!*

I KNOW WE'VE BEEN BUSY CAMPAIGNING, BUT DID YOU *VOTE,* DAD?

D'OH!

JEEZ, HOMER. EVEN *I* VOTED. LOVE THAT *FAKE I.D.*

SO HOW DO WE *RESOLVE* THIS?

I VOTED

I THINK I KNOW...

THE END

LISA'S Historical Dream

OH, MALIBU STACY, I *CAN'T BELIEVE* I'M NOT READY FOR TOMORROW'S {YAWN} *HISTORY TEST!* MUST {YAWN} STUDY MORE OR IT'LL RUIN MY RECORD OF STRAIGHT A'S.

SCRIPT	PENCILS	INKS	LETTERS	COLORS	EDITS	HISTORY CHANNELER
NEIL ALSIP	AARON ROZENFELD	MIKE ROTE	CHRIS UNGAR	ART VILLANUEVA	BILL MORRISON	MATT GROENING

"HISTORY'S GONNA RUIN ME...RUIN ME... RUIN ME...ZZZZZ..."

WAKE UP, LITTLE GIRL.

THANKS, GRAMPA. I'VE GOT A *BIG* TEST TODAY.

GRAMPA? I'M *BENJAMIN FRANKLIN*, DAD BURN IT! NOW, *BEAT IT* WHILE I DISCOVER ELECTRICITY.

EUREKA!

ZZZZT!

MOM, I THINK GRAMPA'S MIXING HIS MEDICATION AGAIN.

I WOULDN'T KNOW ANYTHING ABOUT THAT. I'M *MARIE ANTOINETTE* AND I'M ABOUT TO BE *BEHEADED* BY FRENCH REBELS.

I'M *DEAD*.

FRENCH REBELS?!

YOU'RE NOT MAKING ANY SENSE! IF YOU'RE *REALLY* MARIE ANTOINETTE, THEN HOW DID YOU GET TO SPRINGFIELD?

THE *PAST MASTER*, OF COURSE.

I'M GONNA NEED SOME *STEEL WOOL* FOR THESE STAINS...

WHAT'S GOING ON? WHO *ARE* ALL YOU PEOPLE?!

MY NAME'S *OG*. I INVENTED *FIRE*...OH, AND MALT LIQUOR.

I'M *QUEEN VICTORIA*. AND I PLAN TO *MARRY* THIS OG FELLOW.

I'M *CONFU-DIDDLY-UCIUS*!

I'M...ER...*POPE PIUS THE TWELFTH*??!! OY! HAVE THEY GOT *THAT* WRONG!

I'M *MARIE CURIE* AND I EAT *RADIUM*!

I'M *GANDHI*, REVERED PACIFIST AND LIBERATOR OF INDIA.

AND I'M SOME GUY WHO *PUNCHES* GANDHI!

OOF!

SCUSE ME, PARDON ME, PROFESSIONAL PILLAGER COMING THROUGH!

BART!

UM, THAT'S *BARTILLA*. BARTILLA THE HUN!

OKAY...LISTEN, WHAT CAN YOU TELL ME ABOUT THIS *PAST MASTER*?

ALL I KNOW IS, IF I AGREE TO *CHANGE* A FEW BATTLE PLANS, THE PAST MASTER TRADES ME THESE THINGS CALLED "WALKIE-TALKIES". WITH *THAT* KINDA TECHNOLOGY, MY LOOTING NUMBERS'LL TRIPLE! HECK, *IMPALINGS ALONE* HAVE ALREADY *DOUBLED*!

THAT'S *HORRIBLE!* BY MESSING WITH HISTORY, THE PAST MASTER COULD WREAK *HAVOC* ON THE FUTURE!

DID I MENTION IMPALINGS HAVE *DOUBLED?*

PLEASE, BART, HELP ME STOP THE PAST MASTER! DO IT FOR *JUSTICE!* DO IT FOR THE *LOVE OF HUMANITY!*

I WOULD, BUT I PROMISED THIS CAPTIVE I'D DRAG HIM BEHIND MY HORSE FOR A FEW HOURS.

NO, GO WITH HER. REALLY, I DON'T MIND.

HI-*YA!*

AT *LEAST* TELL ME WHERE HE LIVES!

THE BIG PLACE ON MAMMON AVENUE!

PLEASE! I'M ALLERGIC TO *GRAVEL!*

MAMMON AVENUE? WHY, THAT'S...*BURNS'* MANSION!

NOW THAT I'VE CONVINCED THESE HISTORICAL FIGURES TO DO MY BIDDING, I MERELY HIT THE EXECUTE BUTTON AND THE PRESENT SHALL *INSTANTLY* CHANGE TO THE WAY IT *SHOULD* BE. THE WAY *I* WANT IT! THEN THE PARTY CAN *REALLY* START!

1978

SAN FRANCISCO

EXECUTE

I'LL BRING THE DIP, SIR.

WHOA!

WELL, IF IT ISN'T A *MEDDLING MARTHA!* I'LL SEND YOU BACK TO PRE-HISTORY AND LET YOU MEDDLE WITH AN *ANKYLOSAUR!!*

GRR!

I'LL SAVE YOU!

BARTILLA! YOU *CAME*!

ALLEY--

CLICK!

--OOPS!

FINALLY, MY *PERFECT WORLD* IS REALIZED! I GIVE YOU...

"...MONTY LAND!"

GOOD DAY, MONTY.

GOOD DAY TO YOU, MONTY.

TOP O' THE MORNIN' MONTY!

I'LL SEE HER HANGED!

HULLO, MONTY!

HE MUST BE CRUSHED!

GOOD DAY TO *YOU*, MADAM MONTY.

COME ON, JUST ONE MORE STEP...

GOOD DAY, OFFICER O'MONTY.

RIGHT INTO MY TRAP!

WHY IF IT ISN'T MONTY!

SWEET, LITTLE, MONTY!

THAT SWIRLING NEST OF LIES!

TORTURE, *THEN* EVISCERATE? OR JUST EVISCERATE...

I'LL CHOKE THE SEAS WITH THEIR BLOOD!

HUNH?!! THANK GOODNESS IT WAS ALL A *DREAM*! RIGHT, MALIBU STACY?

BIDE YOUR TIME, MALIBU MONTY, BIDE YOUR TIME...

THE END.

M.C. HOMER!

SIMPSONS COMICS

#59

US $2.50
CAN $3.50

HOMER GETS IN SYNCH WITH THE BOY BAND CRAZE!

ERIC ROGERS
STORY

PHIL ORTIZ
PENCILS

TIM BAVINGTON
INKS

ART VILLANUEVA
COLORS

KAREN BATES
LETTERS

BILL MORRISON
EDITOR

MATT GROENING
FORMER HEARTTHROB

AAAAHHHHHH!!!

EEEEEEEEEEEE!

I'VE NEVER FELT SO *ALIVE WITH PLEASURE.*

♪ OOPS, HIT ME ♪ AGAIN, OR IT'S BYE-BYE, BABY! AND I--WANT-- ♪ IT...LIKE THAT!!! ♪

THERE YOU GO, KIDS! THE *BIGGEST* SINGING SENSATION IN THE COUNTRY, *"BOYZ FROM DA 'BURBS"*, SINGING THEIR *NUMBER ONE* HIT SINGLE, *"I WANT IT THAT WAY WITH MY VIDA LOCA GENIE IN A BOTTLE ONE MORE TIME!"*

WE LOVE YOU!

YEEEAAAAH!

YEAH, IT'S GREAT BEING A BIG STAR, ISN'T IT, BOYS? THE *FAME*, THE *FORTUNE*, SEEING THE *WORLD*...

IT *SURE* IS, KRUST--

SURE, THE VIEW FROM *THE TOP* IS GREAT. BUT THEY DON'T TELL YOU HOW IT IS ON THE *WAY DOWN!* PEOPLE FORGET YOUR *NAME*. YOU HAVE TROUBLE BOOKING GIGS IN *TOLEDO*. YOU STOP GETTING THE HYPO-ALLERGENIC CLOWN MAKE-UP FOR *FREE*...

...IN AND OUT OF THE BETTY FORD CLINIC SO MUCH THEY *RESERVE A ROOM* FOR YOU...*UPN SITCOMS*...AND NOW *THIS*, HOSTING A SHOW FOR SNOTTY LITTLE BRATS WHO WOULDN'T KNOW *TALENT* IF IT *PUNCHED* THEM IN THE *THROAT!* YEAH, BEING AN ENTERTAINER IS THE *BEST*.

NOW, HERE'S ANOTHER FREAKIN' CARTOON!

DUDE, I THOUGHT HE WAS SUPPOSED TO *ASK ABOUT THE TOUR!*

AREN'T THEY *DREAMY*?

♪ I'M SINGIN' AND DANCIN', BUT I CAN'T WRITE MY NAME! I MAKE A MILLION BUCKS A DAY, ♪ THOUGH MY SONGS ARE REALLY LAME! ♪♪

MOM! TELL BART TO STOP SHAKING HIS *BUTT* IN MY *FACE*!

IT'S NOT IN YOUR FACE! IT'S JUST IN THE *VICINITY*!

BART, SHAKE YOUR BEHIND SOMEWHERE ELSE.

WHAT'S THE MATTER, LIS? CAN'T HANDLE THE TRUTH THAT YOUR *SUCK-O* BOY BANDS ARE A BUNCH OF *AIR-HEADED PUPPETS*?

OH YEAH? EXPLAIN *TOM GREEN*!

YOU DON'T GET AS *RICH AND FAMOUS* AS THEY ARE WITH-OUT *TALENT*!

WHAT'S ALL THE FIGHTING ABOUT? IS THIS ANOTHER ARGUMENT OVER WHO GETS STUCK WITH DADDY'S *DEBT* WHEN HE'S TOO OLD AND SENILE TO PAY BILLS?

JUST THREE MORE YEARS...MAN, THAT'LL BE SWEET...

NO, MY *FAVORITE GROUP* WAS ON TV, AND BART WAS *MAKING FUN* OF THEM!

THEY'RE *FAKES,* DAD! THEY DON'T WRITE *MUSIC,* THEY CAN'T PLAY *INSTRUMENTS,* AND ALL THEY DO IS *DANCE* AND *LIP SYNCH* THE WORDS! THEY'RE *SOMEBODY ELSE'S* CREATION TO MAKE MONEY OFF *DUMB GIRLS* AND *MILHOUSE!*

WAIT A MINUTE... YOU'RE TELLING ME THIS MUSIC GROUP DOES ALL THE *HARD* WORK WHILE *SOMEONE ELSE* MAKES THE MONEY?

THEY'RE CALLED *"BOY BANDS".* THEY'RE CUTE, HOT, AND TO *DIE* FOR!

"BOY BANDS", EH? I THINK I MIGHT HAVE AN IDEA WORTH *REMEMBERING...*

OH, THIS *FILTHY* LAMP SHADE!

AWW...

WAIT! *YES!* IT *IS* AN IDEA! AN IDEA WITH A *HIP BEAT* THAT YOU CAN *DANCE* TO!

HOMIE, THIS ISN'T ANOTHER *GET-RICH-QUICK* SCHEME, IS IT?

IS THERE *ANOTHER* KIND?

A FEW DAYS LATER...

WOW! THAT'S ALMOST EVERY BOY I'VE EVER SEEN IN SPRINGFIELD!

SPRINGFIELD BOY BAND TRYOUTS AND CAR-WASHING COMPETITION

AND THERE ARE EVEN SOME KIDS I'VE *NEVER* SEEN BEFORE. IT'S ALMOST AS IF THEY'RE THERE TO *FILL SPACE!*

STUPID HYPNOTIC FISH...

NO TIME FOR CHIT-CHAT, LISA. EVERY SECOND WE DON'T HAVE A BOY BAND MAKING US *RICH* IS ANOTHER SECOND I HAVE TO LIVE WITH THE REGRET OF INVESTING YOUR *COLLEGE SAVINGS* IN THAT *SINGING TROUT!*

DAD, YOU DON'T HAVE ANY *EXPERIENCE* MANAGING A BAND. HOW ARE YOU GOING TO *DO* IT?

HONEY, IF THERE'S ONE THING I HOPE I'VE TAUGHT YOU, IT'S THAT SUCCESS IS 95 PERCENT *BLIND NAIVETE* AND 5 PERCENT *OTHER STUFF.*

PLUS, I HAVE *THIS!* THE *BIBLE* FOR EVERY BOY BAND THAT'S EVER *SUCCEEDED!*

WHAP!

OOOOH. DOES IT HAVE ANY *PICTURES?*

WOULD I EVEN *OPEN* A BOOK THAT *DIDN'T?*

TALENT, SCHMALENT: HOW TO BUILD YOUR OWN BOY BAND

by LOU HANDOVARPHIST, JR., MANAGER OF MEGA-SUCCESSFUL BOY GROUPS 'COOKIE-CUT BOYZ' AND N'TOLERABLE.

64

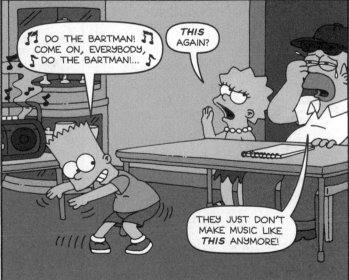

AT THE END OF THE DAY...

ALL RIGHT, EVERYONE. I'VE MADE MY SELECTIONS. I'M GOING TO CALL OUT THE NAMES OF THE PEOPLE WHO MADE THE CUT.

EVERYONE ELSE, THANKS FOR YOUR TIME...IT WAS A REALLY TOUGH DECISION...PLEASE FIND SOMEWHERE OTHER THAN MY FRONT YARD TO BE *JEALOUS* AND *PITIFUL*.

AND THE MEMBERS OF THE SPRINGFIELD BOY BAND ARE...

...NELSON MUNTZ!...

SO DREAMS REALLY *DO* COME TRUE.

...ROD FLANDERS!...

I'M *BLESSED*!

YOU *ALWAYS* GET GOD'S BLESSING!

...BART SIMPSON!...

GET READY, BOYS, 'CAUSE I'M ABOUT TO BECOME EVERY GIRL'S *SECRET CRUSH*!

...AND LASTAMLY... *ROY*!

AYYYYYYYY!

BUT I DETAILED YOUR *HUBCAPS* WITH MY *TOOTHBRUSH*!

UH, DAD, DID ROY EVEN TRY-OUT?

I DON'T KNOW, BUT HE'S JUST *TOO COOL* TO NOT BE IN THE BAND!

DAD, YOU ONLY HAVE *FOUR MEMBERS!* THE BOY BAND BIBLE SAYS YOU *HAVE* TO HAVE *FIVE!*

YES, BUT THEY HAVE TO FIT THE DESCRIPTION OF WHAT EVERY BOY BAND NEEDS...

"THE *EDGY* ONE, THE *BAD BOY,* THE *COOL* ONE, *AND THE BOY NEXT DOOR!*" LEAVING ME WITH ONE GIANT HOLE TO FILL..."THE *FUNNY* ONE!"

AND THE ONLY TIME I LAUGHED DURING THOSE AUDITIONS WAS WHEN MILHOUSE FAKED THAT *ASTHMA ATTACK* DURING HIS SONG.

DAD, THAT WAS *REAL.*

I GAVE HIM *POINTS FOR AUTHENTICITY!*

EXCUSE ME MR. SIMPSON, BUT I BELIEVE *I* DESERVE THE LAST SLOT IN YOUR BOY BAND.

OH YEAH? YOU'VE GOT FIVE SECONDS TO MAKE ME LAUGH--*GO!*

WHAT? BUT I--WHAT AM I--?

YOUR *THREE SECONDS* ARE UP! NO *HA-HA* FOR ME, NO *BOY BAND* FOR YOU!

I TRY TO BE *GENTLE,* I REALLY DO.

SO WHAT *NOW,* DAD?

THE SEARCH FOR THE FIFTH MEMBER CONTINUES...

...AND I KNOW JUST WHERE TO FIND TALENTLESS BOYS DREAMING OF THE GOOD LIFE...

SO APU, ANY SUGGESTIONS? I NEED SOMEONE WHOSE SKELETON IS "ONE GIANT, GYRATING FUNNY BONE."

SORRY, HOMER, BUT DUE TO MY RELIGIOUS BELIEFS, I CANNOT FIND HUMOR IN ANYTHING AT ANYTIME.

WANTED:
FUNNY BOY FOR SPOT IN SOON-TO-BE RICH AND FAMOUS BOY BAND

(DORKS AND VAN HOUTENS NEED NOT APPLY)

DUFF BEER SALE!

HEH, HEH. THAT'S FUNNY.

IT'S USELESS. I'M NEVER GOING TO GET THE CHANCE TO EXPLOIT THE TALENT OF OTHERS FOR MY OWN PERSONAL GAIN! AGAIN!

LOOKING FOR A KID TO FILL OUT YOUR BOY BAND, ARE YA, SIMPSON?

YEAH, BUT NO ONE FITS THE BILL. THE PEOPLE HERE USED TO BE FUNNY, BUT NOT ANYMORE. I DON'T KNOW WHAT'S HAPPENED THESE LAST FEW SEASONS...I MEAN YEARS.

I HEAR YA. BUT I MAY HAVE THE ANSWER TO YOUR PROBLEM. I KNOW JUST THE RIGHT LAD TO MAKE YOUR BAND COMPLETE...

WHO???

MY BOY, RALPH!

RALPH?! WHY SHOULD I LET HIM IN THE GROUP?

OTHER THAN THE FACT THAT BEING AN OFFICER OF THE LAW, I CAN MAKE YOUR LIFE A LIVING HELL OF UNPAID PARKING TICKETS AND MURDER ACCUSATIONS?

THERE IS ALWAYS THAT...

LOOK, SIMPSON, JUST GIVE RALPHIE HIS DAY IN COURT. AND IF YOU STILL DON'T THINK HE FITS THE BILL, I'LL COME UP WITH SOME OTHER WAY TO COERCE YOU!

DEAL!

LATER...

♪ ...THERE WAS LOVE, ALL ♪ AROUND, BUT I NEVER HEARD IT SINGING, NO I NEVER HEARD IT AT ALL, 'TIL THERE WAS ♪ YOOOOOOOOU. ♪

YOU *SEE*, SIMPSON? VOICE LIKE AN ANGEL! IN LIEU OF A *GOOD PRIVATE EDUCATION*, WE PUT OUR MONEY INTO HELPING THE BOY DEVELOP HIS *SINGING CHOPS*!

CLAP! CLAP!

OH, THAT WAS *SOOO GOOD*, RALPHIE! GUESS WHO GETS TO SIT AT THE DINNER TABLE TONIGHT IN HIS *UNDERWEAR*?

THE STRANGE FAT MAN?

CHIEF, THERE'S NO DENYING THE BOY CAN SING. BUT MY BAND DOESN'T NEED *SINGERS*--IT NEEDS SOMEONE *FUNNY*!

FUNNY? WELL, WHY DIDN'T YOU *SAY* SO?

BOY, OPEN YOUR MOUTH AND JUST SAY WHATEVER *POPS* INTO YOUR HEAD.

SINGING MAKES MY BOOGERS VIBRATE!

YOU'RE HIRED! WHA, HA, HA!

NOW WHO *ELSE* GETS TO SIT AT THE DINNER TABLE IN HIS UNDERWEAR?

A FEW DAYS LATER...

HOMER, I JUST WANT TO THANK YOU AGAIN FOR ALLOWING ME THE HONOR OF MANAGING THE GROUP.

WELL, ACCORDING TO THE BOOK HERE, NIGEL, I NEEDED SOMEONE TO BE THE *SCUZ BAG AGENT* MAKING *SHADY DEALS* AND TAKING *MORE* THAN HIS *TEN PERCENT CUT.* YOUR NAME JUST *POPPED* INTO MY HEAD!

I'M FLATTERED.

NOW, WHAT WE NEED TO CREATE IS A *NEW SOUND!* SOMETHING TO *SEPARATE* US FROM THE *COMPETITION.*

SOOOO TEN MINUTES AGO. NO, WHAT I WANT IS SOMETHING NEW AND REVOLUTIONARY...THE *WALL OF BARBER-SHOP SOUND!*

I HEARD *SYNTHESIZED BANJO-FUNK* IS BIG IN EUROPE!

A *BARBERSHOP* BOY BAND? COULD THIS BE THE SOUND THAT AWAITS US AT THE GATES OF HEAVEN?

ONE CAN ONLY *PRAY.*

ALL RIGHT, CHAPS. TIME TO SEE WHAT WE'VE GOT TO WORK WITH. ON MY COUNT, SING "HAPPY BIRTHDAY". ONE, TWO, THREE, FOUR...

♪♫ HAPPY BIRTHDAY TO YOU, HAPPY BIRTHDAY TO YOU... ♫♪

STOP! THAT WAS...*SOMETHING ELSE!*

I'M SPECIAL!

HOMER, WHAT ARE WE GOING TO *DO*? ONLY THE *FUNNY* ONE CAN SING AND HE'S *NOT PAID* TO DO THAT!

DON'T WORRY. THE ANSWERS WE NEED ARE HERE IN CHAPTER 8, "SO YOUR BOY BAND HAS NO TALENT"!

BLAH BLAH BLAH *TYPICAL* BLAH BLAH BLAH *USE OTHER SINGERS* BLAH BLAH BLAH *NO ONE WILL KNOW THE DIFFERENCE*...

WELL? WHAT DID IT SAY?

AS MUCH AS IT PAINS ME TO DO THIS, IT LOOKS AS IF WE'RE GOING TO HAVE TO GO A *VERY UNETHICAL ROUTE* TO MAKE THIS WORK.

HOMER, ETHICS ARE FOR *FOLKSINGERS* AND *CHRISTIAN ROCK BANDS*.

I KNOW. BUT IT JUST MAKES ME *FEEL BETTER* TO *ACT* LIKE I THOUGHT ABOUT IT FOR A *SECOND*.

DON'T WORRY, HOMER. SINCE RALPH IS THE ONLY ONE WHO CAN SING, WE'LL JUST RECORD HIS VOICE IN *FIVE DIFFERENT HARMONIES*. AND NO ONE WILL *EVER* KNOW THE DIFFERENCE!

PLEASE DON'T *EAT THE HEADPHONES*!

HEH, HEH, HEH. HE SURE IS *FUNNY*.

A FEW DAYS LATER...

BOYS, I'VE GATHERED YOU HERE TODAY TO UPDATE YOU ON YOUR PROGRESS--YOU'RE DOING *GREAT!*

BUT WE HAVEN'T *DONE* ANYTHING!

RALPH'S THE *ONLY ONE* WHO'S BEEN IN THE STUDIO!

PRECISELY! AND THE GROUP HAS *NEVER SOUNDED BETTER!*

REMEMBER, THE MOST IMPORTANT FACET OF A BOY BAND IS *IMAGE*. AND NOW WE HAVE TO PICK THE MOST IMPORTANT PART OF THAT IMAGE--*YOUR NAME!*

ALTHOUGH THE BOOK SAYS THAT NO MEMBER OF THE BOY BAND IS ALLOWED TO HAVE AN OPINION ABOUT ANYTHING *EVER*, WE THOUGHT WE'D ALLOW YOU TO COME UP WITH YOUR *OWN* SUGGESTIONS FOR A NAME!

HOW 'BOUT THE *"BUTTKICK BOYS"*?

"BART AND THE OTHERS"?

"THE 5 WISE MEN"?

YOUR THOUGHTS, ROY?

AYYYYYYY!

NOT BAD. IT'S GOT A *NICE RING* TO IT...

I LIKE THE *"SHELBYVILLE ROCKERS"!*

YOU'RE *KILLING* ME, RALPH!

WHAT ABOUT *"5 FROM 'FIELD"*? BECAUSE YOU KNOW, THERE'S *FIVE* GUYS. AND THEY'RE FROM *SPRINGFIELD*...

...THEN AGAIN, MAYBE NOT. ALL RIGHT. I'M GOING HOME FOR THE NIGHT. SEE YA, TOMORROW!

HOW ABOUT *"5 FROM 'FIELD"*?

JOLLY GOOD, CHAP!

AWESOME, MAN!

IT PACKS *PUNCH!*

ONE LAST THING-- THIS ONE NEEDS A *FINELY-SCULPTED BEARD.*

BUT I CAN'T GROW *FACIAL HAIR!*

DO YOU THINK THAT STOPPED *ZZ TOP*? *NONSENSE!*

IS THERE SOMETHING YOU'D LIKE TO SAY, YOUNG MAN?

YES, KENT, I WOULD. I'M HERE TODAY TO ACCUSE "5 FROM 'FIELD'" OF BEING *FAKES!*

DON'T LISTEN TO HIM! HE'S JUST A *LITTLE JEALOUS BABY* WHO COULDN'T *CUT THE CUSTARD!*

NOW PUT A *PACIFIER* IN IT AND WAIT IN LINE LIKE EVERYONE ELSE!

IF "5 FROM 'FIELD'" IS LEGIT, I *DARE* THEM TO SING *RIGHT NOW!*

UH, THEY *CAN'T!* THEY HAVEN'T *WARMED UP!*

NOT TO MENTION THAT WE'RE *ONLY CONTRACTED* TO SIGN AUTOGRAPHS...BESIDES, THIS STORE ISN'T *ZONED* FOR LIVE CONCERTS!

PLUS, THE FUNNY ONE HASN'T TAKEN HIS *MEDICATION!* HE COULD *SNAP* AT ANY MOMENT!

DADDY PUTS MY *RITALIN PILL* IN MY MASHED POTATOES SO I DON'T KNOW IT'S THERE!

YOU *SEE?* THEY WON'T SING BECAUSE THEY *CAN'T!*

HOW ABOUT IT, "5 FROM 'FIELD'"? ARE YOU THE *REAL DEAL,* OR JUST ANOTHER *OUT-OF-SYNC* BOY BAND FROM THE BACK STREETS?

ERRR... UHHH...

ALL *RIGHT!* YOU WANT PROOF? "5 FROM 'FIELD'" WILL DO A *FREE SHOW* AT SPRINGFIELD ELEMENTARY TOMORROW! THEN EVERYONE WILL SEE THE BOYS' TALENTS ONCE AND FOR ALL!

FLIP FLIP

HOOORAAAAY!

THERE YOU HAVE IT. *"HOORAY".*

ALL RIGHT, LADS, THE GAUNTLET'S BEEN HURLED. ALL WE NEED TO DO IS *PRACTICE, PRACTICE, PRACTICE,* AND WE'LL PROVE THAT LITTLE SNOT *WRONG!*

COME ON, BOYS! WE MAY BE RICH, BUT WE'RE FAR FROM *FILTHY* RICH! WHO WANTS TO GET *DIRTY?*

I DO!

AYYYYY!

WE CAN DO IT!

24 HOURS LATER...

WE *CAN'T* DO IT!

IT'S NEVER TOO LATE TO *RUN!* AS A MATTER OF FACT, THAT'S WHAT THE *BOOK* SAYS TO DO IN SITUATIONS LIKE THESE!

NO, HOMER. DESPITE THE *THERAPY-INDUCING HUMILIATION* AND *EGO-CRUSHING FAILURE*, IT'S TIME FOR THE LADS TO *FACE THE MUSIC.*

STAGE DOOR 3

THAT'S THE PROBLEM! THE MUSIC IS *FAKE!*

IS THERE *ANY* WAY AT ALL TO GET THROUGH THIS PERFORMANCE?

WE KNOW OUR DANCE MOVES, BUT RALPH'S THE ONLY ONE WHO CAN SING! AND HE CAN'T SING ALL FIVE PARTS LIVE LIKE HE DID ON THE RECORD!

OH, *I* SEE! PUTTING *YOURSELF* BEFORE THE *REST* OF THE BAND, ARE YOU?

ZIPPERTH MAKE ZIPPING SOUNDTH!

WELL, IT'S ALMOST TIME. GIVE IT YOUR BEST GO, BUCKOS. AND NO MATTER WHAT HAPPENS, JUST REMEMBER THAT *WE BELIEVE IN YOU.*

STAGE DOOR 3

HA, HA.

THEY HAVEN'T GOT A CHANCE, HOMER! LET'S STAND BY THE DOOR SO AS TO BE THE FIRST ONES OUT WHEN THE RIOT BEGINS!

JOHN 3:16

THE FATE OF "5 FROM 'FIELD'" RELIES ON TODAY'S LIVE PERFORMANCE. IF THEY CAN PROVE TO THE WORLD THAT THEY SING THEIR OWN SONGS, THEY CAN LOOK FORWARD TO A LONG CAREER OF 6 MONTHS TO 2 YEARS IN POP MUSIC!

WELL, IT WAS FUN WHILE IT LASTED.

YOU KNOW, I LEARNED SOMETHING FROM ALL OF THIS.

YOU *CAN* LOOK LIKE A *FANCY BOY* AND STILL GET GIRLS.

I'M GONNA MISS THE *CHICKS* AND THE *PARTIES*.

WHAT ABOUT YOU, ROY? ANYTHING *YOU'D* LIKE TO ADD?

AYYYY.

NICE SAVE, RALPH.

THANKS, DUDE. I GUESS I WON'T BEAT YOU UP FOR YOUR *LUNCH MONEY* FOR THE NEXT WEEK OR SO.

THANKTH!

GOOD ONE THERE, RALPHIE. THE OTHERS WERE *HOLDING YOU BACK* ANYWAY!

ABOUT THIS "SOLO CAREER", CHIEF, I SAY WE TAKE RALPH IN AN ENTIRELY NEW DIRECTION. I'M THINKING "SPEED-METAL OPERA"!

I'M OUTTA HERE.

WE'RE LISTENING...

SO, BART, HOW DO YOU FEEL NOW THAT YOU'RE A *NOBODY* AGAIN?

IT'S *GREAT!* I DON'T HAVE TO SCHEDULE *DANCE REHEARSAL* AROUND *SPRAYING GRAFFITI* ON SCHOOL PROPERTY!

SPRINGFIELD BOY BAND BREAKS-UP!

PLUS, MR. SMITHERS IS GOING TO TRADE ME HIS *ENTIRE* "RADIO-ACTIVE MAN" COLLECTION FOR MY "5 FROM 'FIELD" WARDROBE!

BUT THE BEST PART OF ALL IS HOW DESPITE THE *TEMPTATIONS* OF SUCCESS, NONE OF US HAVE CHANGED!

YEAH! IT'S LIKE IT *NEVER EVEN* HAPPENED!

UH, SO ROD, WHO ARE YOUR *NEW FRIENDS?*

TELL "BEYOND THE CHARTS" *YOUR* VERSION OF "FIVE FROM 'FIELD'S" BREAK-UP!

IT'S THE *APOCALYPSE,* DADDY!

ARE YOU MY *TATOO ARTIST?* 'CAUSE THE PICTURE OF *JESUS* ON MY BICEP NEEDS A TOUCH-UP...

THE END

WELL...AH... MR. BURNS, SIR. I GUESS THE *FIRST THING* WE DO IS ANTE UP A BUCK.

INDEED.

CAN ANYONE BREAK A *TEN THOUSAND DOLLAR BILL?*

DO YOU HAVE ANYTHING *SMALLER?*

HMMMM...YES! NO, WAIT, THAT'S A *HUNDRED THOUSAND.* A FIFTY THOUSAND. TWO MORE TENS.

OH, WHY DID I USE ALL MY CHANGE AT THE *LAUNDROMAT?*

TELL YOU WHAT, I'LL BET *SMITHERS.*

WHAT?

WHAT?

WHAT?

WHAT?!!!

UNLESS, ANYONE WOULD LIKE TO QUESTION MY *AUTHORITY.*

NO!

NO!

NO!

NO!!!!

GOTTA LOSE TA BURNSIE.

GOTTA LET THE BOSS WIN.

♪IF YOU WANNA BE MY LOVER, YOU GOTTA GET WITH MY FRIENDS...♪

I FOLD.

YES, BUT THE **MONARCHY** JUST ISN'T AS **STABLE** AS IT USED TO BE. IT WAS **TOO RISKY**.

YOU **WHAT?** YOU HAD **THREE QUEENS** AND **TWO KINGS!**

YOU LOST ME OVER **THREE DOLLARS!**

BUT I GAVE **MY WORD** TO THESE FELLOWS. AS MY LOYAL ASSISTANT YOU'RE **HONOR BOUND** TO SERVE WHOEVER WINS THIS HAND.

HONOR BOUND. YES, SIR.

HOMER'S GOT A **FLUSH**. HE WINS!

D'OH!

SO, NOW THAT I'M YOUR ≡SHUDDER≡ **PERSONAL ASSISTANT**, WHAT IS IT YOU ACTUALLY **DO** AROUND HERE?

YOU EVER WATCH "THE JETSONS?"

YES.

PRETTY MUCH THE **SAME JOB** AS GEORGE.

WHOA! WHOA! WHOA!

SMITHERS! STOP THIS CRAZY THING!

WHY DON'T YOU JUST SIT HERE, AND I'LL DO **EVERYTHING** YOUR JOB REQUIRES. JUST STAY OUT OF MY WAY.

SOUNDS GOOD. NOW IF THERE'S NOTHING ELSE YOU NEED, I'M GONNA **PASS OUT**.

WAKE ME AT **QUITTING TIME**.

IT SEEMS SIMPSON'S *OFFICIAL JOB* IS SAFETY INSPECTOR.

LEAKS, CORE BREACHES, DEPRESSED WORKERS, AND 35% MORE MUTANTS THAN THE GOVERNMENT ALLOWS. I HAD *NO IDEA!*

MR. BURNS, SIR...

EXCUSE ME? AND YOU ARE?

WAYLON SMITHERS, SIR. I WAS YOUR *PERSONAL ASSISTANT* FOR THE *LAST TWO DECADES*. YOU LOST ME TO SIMPSON THIS MORNING.

SIMPSON'S MAN, EH? WELL, GO ON. I HAVEN'T GOT *ALL DAY*.

I HAVE A LIST OF *SAFETY VIOLATIONS* AND THEIR REPAIR COSTS TRIPLE COLLATED AND INDEXED WITH A *WITTY FOREWORD* BY DENNIS MILLER.

THESE CHANGES WOULD COST ME *MILLIONS!* AND MILLER USED THE SAME KIERKEGAARD REFERENCE *TWICE*. YOU *AND* SIMPSON ARE *FIRED*. AND COUNT YOURSELF LUCKY THE OFFICE TRAP DOOR IS BEING *CLEANED* TODAY.

WE FOUND THE *CLOG*. IT'S THE ACTRESS WHO PLAYED FLO ON THE 1970s TV SHOW "*ALICE*."

YES, I REMEMBER! WELL, POLLY HOLIDAY, WHO'S KISSING WHOSE GRITS, NOW?

TRAP DOOR SNAKE

SOON...

I...I JUST CAN'T TELL YOU HOW *SORRY* I AM.

RELAX. IF I DIDN'T GET FIRED *EVERY FEW WEEKS*, I'D *NEVER* GET TO SEE THE KIDS.

I'M STILL HONOR BOUND TO BE YOUR ASSISTANT.

KNOCK YOURSELF OUT.

SO, HOMER, WILL MR. SMITHERS BE STAYING FOR DINNER?

YEAH, SURE, WHATEVER. HEY, HOW ABOUT A *BEER*?

HERE YOU GO, HOMIE.

THERE YOU ARE, SIR. AN *IMPORTED* GERMAN "HERR DUFF" MICROBREW IN A *FROSTED MUG*.

THANKS, MR. SMITHERS.

CALL ME WAYLON.

HRRMMM...

YO, HOW COME HOMER GETS *FILET MIGNON*, AND WE GET *CANNED LIVER*?

AND *TOFU LIVER SUBSTITUTE*.

BECAUSE HOMER'S ASSISTANT SAID IT WASN'T *GOOD ENOUGH* FOR HIM. RIGHT, HOMER?

MMMM! CAN'T TALK! *BEST MEAL* I'VE EVER EATEN. ‡GULP!‡

SORRY, BUT IT'S *MY DUTY* TO MAKE SURE MR. SIMPSON EATS *PROPERLY* AND THAT MEANS AVOIDING *THIRD RATE COOKING*.

HRRMMM...

LATER THAT NIGHT...

LISTEN HOMER, I KNOW YOU LIKE HAVING AN ASSISTANT, BUT I SOME- TIMES FEEL LIKE I'M *COMPETING* WITH HIM FOR YOUR *APPROVAL.*

I KNOW. ISN'T IT *GREAT?*

ALMOST DONE WITH THE WINDOWS, THEN I'LL TUCK YOU IN.

I'LL BE WAITING.

HRRRMMM!!

THE NEXT DAY...

CONFOUND IT, WHERE'S MY FILE CABINET? AND THE WATER COOLER? AND MY ROLODEX OF *BRIBEABLE* JUDGES?

MONTGOMERY BURNS

NO IFS, ANDS, OR BUTS. I *NEED* A PERSONAL ASSISTANT, AND I'M GOING TO *HIRE* THE *NEXT PERSON* I SEE.

WHAT ARE *YOU* DOING HERE?

DOES IT MATTER?

NOT REALLY. *YOU'RE HIRED!*

MONTGOMERY BURNS

MEANWHILE...

I'M HOME FROM THE GROCERY STORE!

WHAT'S THIS? THE REFRIGERATOR IS *FULL*!

I TOOK THE LIBERTY OF BUYING THIS WEEK'S FOOD.

I ALSO HAD THE CARPETS STEAMED AND YOUR PETS SPAYED AND NEUTERED.

NOW YOU LISTEN TO ME, MISTER! I...

HELLLLLO! I FEEL *SNACKISH*!

IF YOU'LL EXCUSE ME, MY HUSBAND *NEEDS* ME.

I MADE YOUR *FAVORITE* THIS MORNING, HOMEY. *DOUBLE FUDGE CARAMEL SQUARES*.

MMM...

BUT MAYBE YOU'D PREFER *BACON* IN A *CHOCOLATE FONDUE*.

¡GASP!¡

MARGE, THE FONDUE AND I WOULD LIKE TO BE *ALONE* FOR A FEW MINUTES.

OH, HOMER! ¡SOB!¡

BACK AT THE PLANT...

SO THE JOB IS PRETTY MUCH *TOADYING* 24-7? DOESN'T SEEM LIKE MUCH FUN.

OH, IT'S NOT ALL *BOOTLICKING*, MY BOY. YOU'LL ALSO BE *HOBNOBBING* WITH *SPRINGFIELD'S ELITE*.

SPEAKING OF WHICH. IT'S TIME FOR OUR WEEKLY GET TOGETHER!

WOW, KRUSTY! RAINIER WOLFCASTLE! AND...SOME GUY I'VE NEVER SEEN.

I'M RANDY SCHOOLEY. I HAVE A *NEW SERIES ON FOX* THIS FALL ABOUT A GUY FROM *ATLANTIS* WHO TEACHES TROUBLED HIGH SCHOOL STUDENTS.

IT'S CALLED *"BELOW C LEVEL"*.

OH, YES. MR. MURDOCH WANTED ME TO PASS A MESSAGE ALONG TO YOU. YOUR SHOW IS ON *HIATUS*.

ANY CHANCE I'LL BE PICKED UP BY THE *SPRING*?

FUNNY YOU SHOULD MENTION THAT.

YAAAAAH!

SPROING!

HEY, HEY! NOW THAT THE NO-BODY'S GONE, WE'LL MEET YOU IN THE BASEMENT.

BUT HURRY UP. DAT *BEAR* WON'T *BAIT* ITSELF.

BART, I'LL BE BUSY FOR THE REST OF THE DAY. OH, BUT I MADE A FEW CALLS. THIS IS FOR YOU. USE IT WHENEVER YOU GET INTO *TROUBLE*.

DIPLOMATIC IMMUNITY?

SO AS MUCH AS I'D LOVE TO STAY FOR DETENTION...

SINCE WHEN DID YOU BECOME *AMBASSADOR TO KENYA?*

"EXCUSE ME, MR. SMITHERS...?"

THERE'S A *MOVING VAN* OUT FRONT. NOW ENOUGH IS *ENOUGH!*

I'VE PUT MOST OF MY THINGS IN *STORAGE*, BUT I JUST COULDN'T STAND TO BE AWAY FROM MY *MALIBU STACY COLLECTION*.

I'LL BE DONE *ALPHABETIZING* THEM IN TWO SHAKES OF A LAMB'S TAIL.

I'VE BEEN MORE THAN PATIENT WITH YOUR _HUSBAND-USURPING_, BUT THIS IS GOING _TOO FAR!_

I KNOW. IT'S _STRANGE_. AT FIRST THE IDEA OF BEING HOMER'S ASSISTANT _REPULSED_ ME. BUT I HAVE TO ADMIT HE _GROWS ON YOU_. AND IF I DON'T TAKE CARE OF HIM, WHO WILL?

THAT'S _MY_ JOB!

AFRAID OF A LITTLE _HEALTHY COMPETITION?_

AFRAID OF _YOU_? HA! WE'LL JUST SEE WHO'S _THE BETTER WIFE!_

FINE. NOW BE A DEAR AND CLOSE THE DOOR ON YOUR WAY OUT. TOO MUCH _HUMIDITY_ IS BAD FOR THE GIRLS.

"OKAY, MR. BURNS..."

...IT TOOK AN _HOUR_, BUT YOUR {UGH!} TOENAIL IS _CLIPPED_.

GOOD LAD. LUCKY THEY ALL _FUSED TOGETHER_ INTO _ONE NAIL_ YEARS AGO. MAKES FOR A _QUICKER JOB_.

YEAH, LUCKY.

LOOK AT THESE _SLUGGARDS_ DRAGGING THEIR CARCASSES AROUND MY BEAUTIFUL PLANT. THEY _SICKEN_ ME.

MAYBE YOU SHOULD MAKE WORK _MORE FUN_.

FUN. YES, THAT WOULD LURE THEM INTO A _FALSE SENSE OF SECURITY_. GO ON WITH THIS "_FUN_" PLAN OF YOURS.

HOW ABOUT _PAINTBALL?_

WITH ONLY _MY_ GUN CONTAINING _ACTUAL BULLETS_. EXCELLENT.

MAYBE THEY SHOULD _ALL HAVE_ PAINT.

HMMM...FINE, FINE. MAKE IT SO.

NOW BE A GOOD LAD AND _SAND MY BACK_.

"THERE! ALL OF HOMER'S LAUNDRY IS DONE."

FRESH AND HOT FROM THE DRIER WITH AN *EXTRA DOSE* OF SOFTENER!

MARGE, COME QUICK!

OH MY LORD! HOMER, WHAT *HAPPENED* TO YOU?

WAYLON MADE ME A *NEW OUTFIT!* PRETTY *SNAZZY,* HUH?

IT'S SIMPLE *QUANTUM SEWING MATHEMATICS.* THE CLOTHES *REDISTRIBUTE MASS* GIVING A *SLIMMER LOOK.*

THAT'S WONDERFUL. LET'S *CELEBRATE* WITH THIS BUCKET OF *EXTRA KRUSTY CHICKEN.*

NO! THE CLOTHES CAN'T TAKE THE *PRESSURE!*

MMM... CHICKEN!

SHRED!

¡CHEW!¡ ¡GULP!¡

OF COURSE YOU KNOW, THIS MEANS *WAR!*

LATER THAT DAY...

IT SEEMS TO BE GOING WELL.

THE CAN SAYS THIS PAINT SHOULD BE USED ONLY IN A *WELL-VENTILATED* AREA.

VENTILATION? PISH AND TOSH! WHY DON'T I GET *REAL LEAD* IN THE REACTOR LEVEL SAFETY DOORS WHILE WE'RE *THROWING MONEY AWAY?*

JUST A BIT OF *FRIENDLY ADVICE*, MARGE. YOU COULD GET MORE DONE IN A DAY IF YOU HAD A *MORE EFFICIENT HAIRCUT*.

OH REALLY?

I HAVE A NUMBER FIVE FLATTOP. THE *FASTEST HAIR CUT* KNOWN TO MAN.

IGOR
the magazine for assistants

Naggers Monthly

AND, JUST BETWEEN US, THE ADDED HAIR HEIGHT MAKES YOUR *HIPS* LOOK *HUGE*.

WHY YOU--!

OH MY HEAVENS! WHAT A *CAT FIGHT!*

HISS!

SCRATCH!

SOMEONE SHOULD STOP THAT BEFORE THE TWO KITTIES GET HURT.

OPEN

PFFT!

RWOWWR!

PFFT!

I'LL DO IT. I'VE FINISHED MY HAIRCUT ALREADY.

BESIDES, I NEED TO GET HOME. I RENTED HOMER'S FAVORITE CYBORG COWBOY GORILLA MOVIE, SO HE HAS SOMETHING TO WATCH DURING HIS *MASSAGE*.

GRRRRRRR...

SUPPORT YOUR LOCAL

ROBO CHIMP!

A FEW DAYS LATER...

YOUR SUGGESTION OF *FREE SODAS* AND *VIDEO GAMES* SEEMS TO BE A HIT WITH THE DRONES.

AND SO YOU SHALL, RIGHT AFTER YOU DO MY *TAXES* FOR THE LAST FIVE YEARS AND GIVE ME A THOROUGH *EAR HAIR WAXING*.

I SAID *I* WANTED A SODA AND TO GO PLAY VIDEO GAMES WITH MILHOUSE.

DASH DINGO

DASH DINGO

SORRY, SIR. I THOUGHT YOU'D *PASSED OUT* FROM DRINKING.

OH, RIGHT. THE *BREAKFAST BEER BURRITO EXPERIMENT.*

SAY, WHY'S YOUR ROOM LOOK LIKE LISA'S?

THIS IS MY MALIBU STACY COLLECTION. *MY PRIDE AND JOY.*

WHAT'S ALL THIS JUNK?

THAT'S STACY'S JAGUAR. I ALSO HAVE HER DREAM CONDO, HER LIPOSUCTION CLINIC AND MY FAVORITE...HER *BULB & BAKE OVEN.*

IT REALLY *WORKS!* IT USES A 500-WATT BULB TO COOK MINI-TREATS EXTRA QUICK.

WOULD YOU LIKE ME TO MAKE YOU A RHUBARB TART?

MAYBE LATER.

☆Stacy☆ BULB and BAKE OVEN

WELL, IF YOU DON'T NEED ANYTHING I'M GOING TO THE STORE FOR MORE *DOLL POLISH.*

YOU DO THAT.

"JUST LOOK AT IT, BART!"

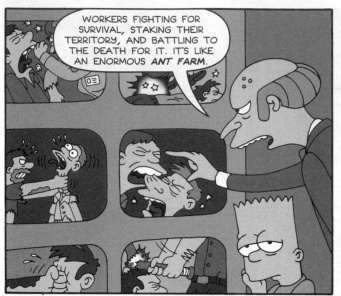

WORKERS FIGHTING FOR SURVIVAL, STAKING THEIR TERRITORY, AND BATTLING TO THE DEATH FOR IT. IT'S LIKE AN ENORMOUS *ANT FARM.*

ESPECIALLY SECTOR 4-G WITH THE *GIANT MUTATED ANTS.*

YEAH, IT'S GREAT. Y'KNOW, I CAN'T BELIEVE I'M SAYING THIS, BUT I HAVE *HOMEWORK* I SHOULD BE DOING.

INDEED, RIGHT AFTER YOU TEACH ME EVERYTHING THERE IS TO KNOW ABOUT *THE INTERNET* AND POP MY *KNEE-CAPS* BACK INTO PLACE.

MEN

HEY! AN *UNOPENED SODA!* MORE PRECIOUS THAN *GOLD!*

WE'VE TRAPPED THEIR LEADER. NOW KING CARL RULES *ALL!*

LAY-OFFS

MEN

MAN, AFTER ALL THAT SODA I REALLY HAVE TO GO TO THE BATHROOM.

WISH WE'D LOCKED HIM IN THE *REACTOR CORE.*

"NOW HOW DOES THIS WORK AGAIN?"

HMMM... LET'S SEE...

UH, OH!

LATER...

THANKS FOR LOOKING AFTER MY BABIES FOR ME, HOM—

AAAAAAH!

HEY, WAYLON. *FUNNY STORY*. WELL, NOT SO MUCH FUNNY TO YOU, BUT...

UM, WAYLON? ARE YOU ALL RIGHT?

THE NAME IS *MISTER SMITHERS!*

I WENT THROUGH A LOT WORKING FOR MR. BURNS, BUT AT LEAST HE NEVER *DEFILED* MY GIRLS. HOMER'S ALL YOURS! YOU WIN! *I QUIT!*

MR. BURNS, I PROMISED ON MY HONOR THAT I'D WORK FOR HOMER SIMPSON. I'VE *FAILED* YOU.

NOT AT ALL. THAT HONOR AND INTEGRITY OF YOURS WERE YOUR ONLY REAL *FLAWS*.

NOW THAT THEY'RE GONE WE CAN HAVE SOME *REAL FUN* AROUND HERE.

SHOULD I GET YOUR *FORECLOSING SUIT* READY, SIR?

YES, THOSE *WAR ORPHANS* HAVE BEEN *LATE* ON THEIR *RENT* ONE TOO MANY TIMES.

IT'S GOOD TO BE BACK, SIR.

"I'M FIRED?"

FINE! THAT JOB WAS A *STONE COLD DRAG,* ANYWAY! IF I NEVER *BUFF* ANOTHER *BEDSORE* AGAIN, IT'LL BE TOO SOON!

PHONE BOOK

A-HA! I HEARD THAT! YOUR DIPLOMATIC IMMUNITY IS *GONE!*

RATS!

UNLESS...

WE HAVE A FAX FROM BART SIMPSON. HE CLAIMS TO BE HELD AS A *POLITICAL PRISONER* FOR HIS *ANARCHISTIC VIEWS.* HERE ARE HIS PAPERS.

AMBASSADOR OF BUTTSVILLE, ASSACHUSETTS?

AMNESTY INTERNATIONAL

SIR, I'VE REPLACED ALL THE SODA WITH AN UNCAFFEINATED, SUGAR-FREE BRAND, AND THE WORKERS ARE *BACK TO NORMAL.*

C. MONTGOMERY BURNS

"EXCEPT FOR LENNY WHO WAS MADE *QUEEN* OF *SECTOR 4-G.*"

GIVEN *FANTASTIC POWERS* DURING A *FREAK X-RAY ACCIDENT*...

CHILDREN! *DUCK AND COVER* LIKE WE DID DURING THOSE *FREAK X-RAY ACCIDENT DRILLS!*

KA-ZAP!

BART AND LISA SIMPSON BECAME...

STRETCH DUDE
AND
CLOBBER GIRL

LIKE, OW!

NOTHING CAN STOP *THE MINI MISS OF MIGHT* AND *THE RADICAL RUBBER REBEL* IN THEIR *WAR ON CRIME!*

NOTHING EXCEPT...

IF YOU'RE GOING OUT, TAKE *MAGGIE* WITH YOU.

BUT MOM!

IAN BOOTHBY
STORY

PHIL ORTIZ
PENCILS

TIM BAVINGTON
INKS

ART VILLANUEVA
COLORS

KAREN BATES
LETTERS

BILL MORRISON
EDITOR

MATT GROENING
FREAK ACCIDENT INVESTIGATOR

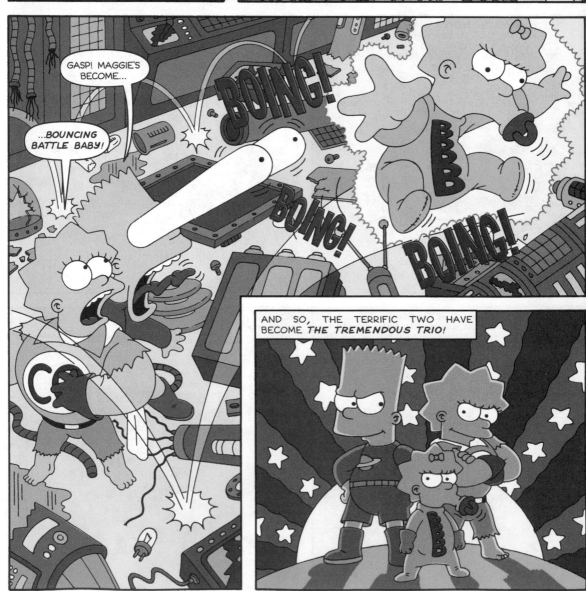

LOOK OUT *EVIL*! *HERE THEY COME*!

UH, LISA? LITTLE HELP?

DO *YOU* WANT TO *CHANGE* HER?

NO! NO! THAT'S OKAY!

UM...NORMALLY WE'D *BEAT YOU UP*, BUT COULD YOU JUST LEAVE? YOU'RE *SCARING* OUR SISTER.

YEAH, SURE.

SORRY ABOUT THAT.

I SEE IT, MR. MAYOR, BUT WE HAVE TO *WAIT* UNTIL MAGGIE FINISHES HER *NAP*.

THAT'S IT. HAVING MAGGIE ON OUR TEAM *BITES*! I WISH SHE'D NEVER *GOT* SUPER POWERS!

THE NEXT DAY...

BART! THERE'S A *ROBBERY* AT THE FOURTH NATIONAL BANK!

WHAT'S THE POINT IN GOING? *RUBBER BABY BATTLE BLOWER* HERE'S ONLY GOING TO *MESS THINGS UP* AGAIN.

OKAY, GIVE ME ALL YOUR *MONEY!* I'M LIKE, TOTALLY ROBBING YOU.

YOU AND WHAT *ARMY!*

THIS ARMY, DUDE!

GIVEN *SUPERPOWERS* IN A *FREAK ELECTRIC CHAIR ACCIDENT,* CRIMINAL SUB-MASTERMIND SNAKE HAS BECOME *SNAKESKIN*...A VILLAIN WITH THE ABILITY TO *SHED HIS SKIN,* CREATING *PERFECT DUPLICATES!*

OH MY GOSH, BART! HOW DO WE KNOW WHICH IS THE *REAL* BANK ROBBER?

MAGGIE! NOT NOW! WE'RE BUSY!

MAN! AND I THOUGHT YOU WERE A *PAIN* WHEN YOU USED TO *HIDE* MY *SLINGSHOT* FOR ATTENTION.

SLINGSHOT? MAGGIE! *THAT'S IT!*

BART THIS IS *CRAZY.*

JUST LET GO ALREADY! YOU'RE GIVING ME A *WEDGIE!*

THERE'S *NO SUCH THING* AS A KITE-EATING TREE, DORKUS!

{WOO-HOY!} NO ONE MUST EVER KNOW ABOUT MY {GAH-HAY} *FAILED* BOTANICAL EXPERIMENTS, THE KITE-EATING TREE...

"...THE *SKATEBOARD-EATING BUSH*..."

"...AND THE {GAH-FLAVEN} *BEER DRINKING MOSS!*"

I SWEAR IT WAS THE *BAR STOOL* THAT DRANK 'EM. I SWITCHED TO LATTES!

I BELIEVE YA, BARN'. THAT'LL BE *SEVENTY-FIVE BUCKS.*

{BRAAAPP!}

HEY, MILHOUSE! WHERE HAVE YOU BEEN?

NO TIME FOR FUN, BART. I GOT A *PAPER ROUTE* TO RAISE MONEY TO GO TO *VIDEO GAME CAMP.*

IT'S THE ONLY CAMP THAT PROMISES ABSOLUTELY *NO FRESH AIR* OR *EXERCISE.*

THAT'S COOL OF YOUR DAD TO *HELP* YOU OUT.

ACTUALLY, HE'S GOT HIS *OWN* ROUTE. MOM CUT OFF HIS ALIMONY.

I'D BETTER NOT CATCH YOU WORKING *MY SIDE* OF THE STREET!

LISTEN, MILHOUSE. BE A PAL AND GIVE ME A COUPLE OF PAPERS TO MAKE A *NEW KITE* WITH!

OH NO, BART! DELIVERING PAPERS IS A *SACRED TRUST*.

BUT THIS IS TIME YOU COULD SPEND BECOMING A *DOT COM BILLIONAIRE*. YOU THINK *BILL GATES* WOULD BE IN COURT TODAY IF HE'D *WASTED HIS TIME* DELIVERING PAPERS?

HARD, POINTLESS WORK IS FOR GUYS LIKE *ME*! JUST HAND OVER THE PAPERS, AND I'LL DELIVER THEM FOR YOU.

OKAY, I... *WAIT!* YOU'RE JUST SAYING THAT SO I'LL *GIVE* YOU THE PAPERS FOR YOUR *KITE!*

MILHOUSE, I DON'T WANT TO *LIE* TO YOU.

YES, YOU DO!

OKAY! OKAY! I DON'T WANT YOU TO *KNOW* I'M LYING TO YOU!

ALL RIGHT! I'LL GIVE YOU THE SUNDAY PAPER *ADVERTISING INSERTS*, BUT THAT'S ALL!

DEAL!

A HALF HOUR LATER...

THANKS, MAN!

WOW! I CAN CARRY A *HUNDRED* PAPERS WITH *ONE HAND*, NOW! I'M A *SUPERHERO!*

WELL, IF IT ISN'T JOSEPH AND HIS AMAZING TECHNI-COLOR DREAM KITE!

COOL, MAN!

MOST SPLENDIFEROUS!

BUT WHAT BART DIDN'T KNOW WAS THAT *OLD MAN WINTER* HAD BEEN SAVING UP A *NASTY WIND* FOR JUST SUCH AN OCCASION.

WHO ARE YOU TALKING TO, GRAMPA?

UM... NOBODY.

CAN'T... HOLD ON!

MUST... LET GO!

WOOSH!

KWIK-E-MART

CHILI DOGS 16 FOR $1 (AS IS)

ONLY *ONE PAPER* TO GO! *NOTHING* CAN STOP MILHOUSE, NOW!

WHAAAAAAA...

GASSO

THIS IS ARNIE PIE WITH YOUR TRAFFIC REPORT. THINGS LOOK GOOD ON ALL THE MAJOR HIGHWAYS, AND IT SHOULD BE SMOOTH SAILING FOR COMMUTERS.

THIS REPORT IS BROUGHT TO YOU BY *DR. WOLFE'S PAINLESS DENTISTRY.* JUST ONE VISIT AND YOU'LL SAY...

AAAAAAH!

OH, DEAR GOD! *NO!*

YAAAA! HELP! NOOOOO!

HRMMMMMM. MAYBE I'LL PUT OFF THIS *ROOT CANAL* A BIT LONGER.

LATER...

MORE SOUP, DEAR?

NO THANKS, MOM.

GEEZ, MILHOUSE, WITH THAT *SPRAINED ANKLE* I GUESS YOU WON'T BE ABLE TO AFFORD TO GO TO CAMP NOW, HUH?

I *CAN* IF YOU *TAKE OVER* MY PAPER ROUTE.

MILHOUSE, I'D *LIKE* TO TELL YOU I'LL BE TAKING OVER YOUR PAPER ROUTE.

PERHAPS YOU'D LIKE TO CONTINUE THIS DISCUSSION WITH *MY ATTORNEY.*

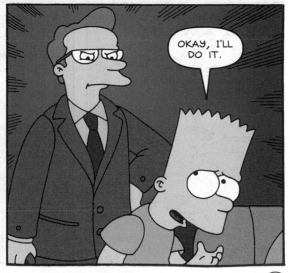

OKAY, I'LL DO IT.

BY ATTACHING EACH PAPER TO A *ROCKET* THE NEWS WILL DELIVER ITSELF!

UM...BART, THESE ARE JUST *ILLEGAL FIREWORKS* DAD BOUGHT FROM THAT POLICE AUCTION.

SORRY I WAS BUSY LIGHTING THE FUSE. DID YOU SAY SOMETHING?

RUN!!!

SHOOM!

BLAM!

WHAT'S THIS? *CONFETTI?* JUST FOR COMING HOME?

HEY, THANKS!

WHAT'S GOING ON? IS IT A *PARTY?* WHY DIDN'T OL' GIL GET AN INVITE?

HOMER SEEMS TO KNOW. LET'S *FOLLOW* HIM!

UM...ER...WHY IS THERE A *PARADE* FOR *THAT* FAT BOOB?

I'M THE MAYOR! I CAN'T APPEAR TO BE *OUT OF THE LOOP!* GIVE ME THE...ER...AH... PHONE.

I DON'T KNOW, SIR.

ALL THOSE MONTHS OF *TRAINING* YOU HAVE PAID OFF! FINALLY, A RESCUE NOTE!

OH, DEAR. IT'S JUST A PEANUT BUTTER SOAKED NEWSPAPER.

I WONDER IF I'M STILL *ALLERGIC* TO NUTS.

I GUESS SO.

NO *PLAN D*?

NAW! IF HOMER'S TAUGHT ME *ONE THING* IT'S "KNOW WHEN TO GIVE UP."

BUT AT LEAST WE *DON'T* HAVE TO GO TO SCHOOL TODAY BECAUSE OF THE *GAS LEAKS.*

WHAT? OH MAN!

SCHOOLS NOT CLOSED

GAS LEAKS FIXED CLAIMS PROUD SCOTSMAN

OH MAN, WHAT?

UM... *NOTHING.*

HEY LIS', CAN I BORROW YOUR *WHITE OUT*?

SURE. WHAT FOR?

A SCHOOL-RELATED PROJECT.

OKAY, I'VE DELIVERED PAPERS TO ALL THE *TEACHERS' HOMES*. PRINCIPAL SKINNER IS THE *LAST* ONE.

WHAT'S THIS? SCHOOLS *CLOSED*?

BUT WHY WASN'T *I* TOLD?

SEYMOUR! CLOSE THAT DOOR! I'M NOT PAYING TO HEAT THE YARD.

ACTUALLY, *I* PAY THE GAS BILL, MOTHER!

WHAT'S THAT? IS THAT *SASS* I HEAR IN YOUR VOICE?

NO, MOTHER.

I DON'T UNDERSTAND. IT'S TEN O'CLOCK. WHERE ARE ALL THE TEACHERS?

DID AN OCTOPUS EAT THEM?

FRIENDS, BULLIES, KIDS I NEVER BOTHERED TO GET TO KNOW. *LEND ME YOUR EARS!*

THERE WILL BE *NO LEARNING* TODAY THANKS TO ME, *BART SIMPSON!*

HOORAY!

WAY TO GO BART!

YAY!

WHY ARE THOSE CHILDREN...ER...UM... CELEBRATING?

I DON'T KNOW, SIR.

I KEEP TELLING YOU, I'M JUST THE *JANITOR*. NOW DO YOU WANT ME TO PUT SAWDUST ON THAT VOMIT OR WHAT?

I CONTROL THE NEWS. I HAVE *TOTAL POWER*. BUT I CAN'T LET IT *CORRUPT* ME.

CAN I CARRY YOUR BOOKS, BART?

CAN I CARRY YOUR BOOKS, BART, *SIR!*

DADDY, HAVE YOU SEEN OUR *LI'L NEWSMAKER PRINTING PRESS?* IT'S *MISSING*.

SORRY, BOYS, I HAVEN'T. NOW GET READY FOR YOUR NIGHTLY BATH.

YAY! EVERY BATH IS LIKE A *MINI-BAPTISM*.

Church Bulletin
PSALMS AND HOW TO PRONOUNCE IT

SWEET!

HERE'S AN *EARLY EDITION* OF THE PAPER, APU. THOUGHT YOU MIGHT LIKE TO SEE IT.

THANK YOU. YOU MAY HAVE *ONE ITEM* FROM THE *THREE-CENT BIN* FOR YOUR KINDNESS.

OH, MY GOODNESS!

HEH, HEH, HEH!

Springfield Shopper
DAILY NEWS
ALL KRUSTY CHOCO-KRISPY KRUNCH BARS RECALLED
TOO MUCH POISON SAY EXPERTS

YOU *DELICIOUS TREATS* ARE A LAW-SUIT WAITING TO HAPPEN. TO THE *DUMPSTER* WITH YOU!

WAY TO GO, BART!

MMMM.

I FEAR I'M SITTING ON *BROKEN GLASS.*

MARGE, DID YOU READ ABOUT THE GOVERNMENT'S *MANDATORY CHILD ALLOWANCE* INCREASE?

ONE HUNDRED DOLLARS A WEEK?

OH WELL, THE LAW IS THE *LAW.*

YOU KNOW, I'M REALLY SURPRISED YOU HAVEN'T RATTED ME OUT YET.

WELL, NORMALLY I WOULD HAVE BUT...

...A HUNDRED DOLLARS IS A HUNDRED DOLLARS.

LATER...

OKAY, BART. *THINK.* SO FAR IT'S BEEN *SMALL POTATOES.* WHAT'S THE NEXT STEP?

ADULTS ARE A *SUPERSTITIOUS, COWARDLY LOT.* WHAT WOULD *STRIKE FEAR IN THEIR HEARTS?*

SMASH!

A *MOTH!*

MAN, HOMER HAS GOT TO STOP BUYING GLASS FROM THE *MOVIE STUNTMAN SUPPLY STORE.*

WAIT A MINUTE! *THAT'S IT!*

MR. BROCKMAN, SIR? HAVE YOU SEEN TODAY'S PAPER?

WHAT A STORY. WE *LEAD* WITH THIS!

SHOULDN'T WE *CONFIRM* THIS WITH OUR *OWN* SOURCES?

LOOK, I TOLD YOU WE COULD EITHER HAVE FACT CHECKERS *OR* A NEW CANDY MACHINE, BUT NOT *BOTH*!

NOW GET ME A *NUTRAGEOUS BAR* AND A *LIVE FEED*!

I'M GOING TO THE COMIC BOOK STORE.

PEOPLE OF SPRINGFIELD ARE ASKED TO *STAY INDOORS* AT ALL TIMES TO AVOID *MOTH-RELATED DEATHS.*

GET YOUR *KEESTER* BACK IN HERE! NO SON OF *MINE* IS GOING TO BE A *MOTH MEAL.*

OH, MAN! I *FORGOT.* I'M TRAPPED TOO. NOW I'LL HAVE TO DELIVER PAPERS SAYING EVERY-THING'S *SAFE.*

BUT I *CAN'T* DELIVER NEWSPAPERS IF I'M *STUCK* INSIDE.

D'OH!

SHOULDN'T YOU BE DOING SOMETHING, CLANCY?

NOTHING IN THE LAWBOOKS AGAINST BEING AN INSECT.

SO THAT'S THE...ER...AH... PROBLEM.

GIANT MOTH, YOU SAY?

THE ARMY HAS A PLAN FOR JUST SUCH AN EMERGENCY.

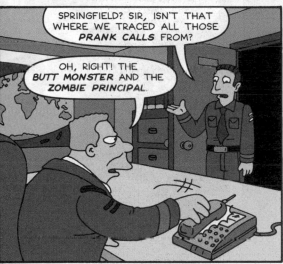

SPRINGFIELD? SIR, ISN'T THAT WHERE WE TRACED ALL THOSE PRANK CALLS FROM?

OH, RIGHT! THE BUTT MONSTER AND THE ZOMBIE PRINCIPAL.

CANCEL THE NUCLEAR MISSILE STRIKE.

HERE I AM, CONFINED TO MY OWN STORE. UNABLE TO HELP MY DEAR WIFE CARE FOR OUR EIGHT TEETHING CHILDREN.

BUT WHAT DO I DO FOR FOOD?

DARE I SAMPLE MY OWN KWIK-E-MART SNACK TREATS FOR THE FIRST TIME?

I CAN'T TAKE BEING *TRAPPED* IN HERE! I'VE DONE EVERY *PUZZLE*, BUILT EVERY MODEL, AND ¬SHUDDER¬ READ EVERY *BOOK* I HAVE.

EVEN *TV* IS *RUINED*.

...AND NOW BACK TO KRUSTY THE CLOWN!

AS YOU KNOW SIDESHOW MEL AND I HAVE BEEN FORCED TO DRINK OUR OWN...*SELTZER*. BUT THE SHOW MUST GO ON. *THROW THAT PIE!*

NO, KRUSTY! *IT'S ALL THE FOOD WE HAVE!*

THE *GAG* COMES *FIRST!*

AS YOU KNOW, WE HAVEN'T BEEN ABLE TO GET ANY *NEW* ITCHY AND SCRATCHY CARTOONS DELIVERED. BUT WE DID FIND AN *OLD EDUCATIONAL FILM* THAT THE SCHOOL SYSTEM COMMISSIONED AND THEN REJECTED. ENJOY LEARNING ABOUT *LONG DIVISION* THE ITCHY AND SCRATCHY WAY.

I GIVE UP, ITCHY. WHAT WILL MY *REMAINDER* BE?

BART YOU'VE GOT TO PUT A *STOP* TO THIS! I'VE READ THE ENCYCLOPEDIA *TWICE*, *DEWEY DECIMALISED* MY BOOKS, AND LEARNED TO PLAY THE *OBOE*.

AAAAAGH!

OKAY, OKAY YOU *WIN!*

MOM, I HAVE SOMETHING TO TELL YOU.

OKAY, BART! HI, LISA!

SAY, WHY AREN'T *YOU* GOING *STIR CRAZY* LIKE THE *REST OF US?*

WELL, I SPEND PRETTY MUCH *ALL DAY* IN HERE ANYWAY, AND IT'S BEEN *NICE* HAVING *COMPANY* TO TALK TO.

AT FIRST, I WAS *WORRIED* ABOUT YOUR *FATHER*...

...BUT HE'S MADE SOME SORT OF *COCOON* OUT OF *JUNK FOOD WRAPPERS* AND HAS GONE INTO *HIBERNATION*. NOW, WHO WANTS TO HEAR THE STORY OF HOW *LISA LOST HER FIRST BABY TOOTH?*

THIS JUST IN...

KENT BROCKMAN IS A *JERK* WHO DIDN'T HAVE A *DATE* UNTIL HE WAS *THIRTY-SIX*.

LATE BREAKING NEWS. SCOTT HAS BEEN *STEALING* FROM THE *COFFEE FUND* AND *SMELLS* REALLY BAD.

ON THE LIGHTER SIDE, KENT'S AN *IDIOT*.

I'M SURPRISED THEY DIDN'T MENTION THE *GIANT MOTH KILLING ROBOT* OUTSIDE.

WHAT?

LISA, I GOTTA GO! THE *CITY* NEEDS ME.

I'LL NEED *COVER.* *YOU KNOW WHAT YOU HAVE TO DO.*

⸱GULP!⸱

MOM, DO YOU HAVE ANY *BABY PICTURES* I COULD LOOK AT?

WHY YES, *YES I DO,* LISA. I'LL MAKE SOME *COCOA,* AND WE CAN *STROLL DOWN MEMORY LANE.*

HER *COURAGE* WILL NOT BE *FORGOTTEN.*

GREAT.

ONE OF THESE *FREQUENCIES* MUST BE RIGHT.

FZZZT!

♪ BACKSTREET'S BACK! ALRIGHT! ♪

OH GOOD GAH—⸱GLAVIN!⸱

THAT'S IT!

SO YOU SEE IT'S ALL BEEN A *MISUNDERSTANDING.* THERE IS *NO* MOTH.

BUT WITH NO MOTH THE *ROBOT* WILL *CONTINUE* ITS *COURSE OF DESTRUCTION* WITH THE *WRATH* AND THE *SMASHING!*

NEW INSECT SPRAY

I'VE GOT IT!

YOU HAVE AN *IDEA?*

NO, I WAS HOPING *HITTING MY HEAD* LIKE THAT WOULD GIVE ME ONE, BUT...

...WAIT! *NOW* I HAVE ONE!

THWAP!

MILHOUSE, WE NEED TO GET TO THE *NEWSPAPER DEPOT,* NOW!

CAN IT WAIT? I'VE ALMOST TAUGHT MYSELF THE THEME FROM "FAME" ON THE *MOUTH HARP.*

OKAY, I'LL HELP. BUT THERE BETTER BE *EXPLOSIONS. BRUCKHEIMER-STYLE EXPLOSIONS!*

WE NEED YOUR *MATH SKILLS* TO HELP BUILD THE *BIGGEST KITE EVER.*

THERE'S A *SLIDE RULER* IN MY POCKET WITH *YOUR* NAME ON IT!

GET THAT *PASTE* OVER HERE.

ATTACH THAT TAIL AT A FORTY-FIVE DEGREE ANGLE.

I NEED A *BEARING PIECE OF BALSA WOOD* ...STAT!

NOT BAD!

BUT WILL IT *FLY?*

ONLY *ONE WAY* TO FIND OUT.

NEW TARGET ACQUIRED.

OH, THANK GOD!

KA-BLAM!

WHOA!

YIKES!

YAAA!

ZOUNDS!

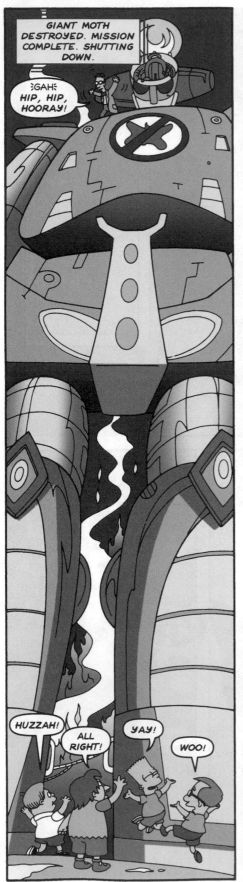

GIANT MOTH DESTROYED. MISSION COMPLETE. SHUTTING DOWN.

EGAH! HIP, HIP, HOORAY!

HUZZAH!

ALL RIGHT!

YAY!

WOO!

AND SO THE CITY WAS *SAVED*, AND BART LEARNED A LESSON ABOUT *TAMPERING* WITH THE NEWS.

OKAY, POPS. WE *WARNED* YOU ABOUT *BOTHERING* THE SQUIRRELS.

AND THE CITY WENT BACK TO *NORMAL*, NONE THE WORSE FOR ITS *ADVENTURE*...

"...WITH A FEW *SMALL* EXCEPTIONS."

APU, *LOOKING GOOD*! HEY, WHERE'S THE CHIPS, CANDY, AND CHOCOLATE?

IT IS MINE, ALL MINE! GET OUT!

THE END

YES, SIR.

NO GATLING GUN! NO MUSTARD GAS! I'D SAY THAT MAKES YOU A PRETTY POOR *GOLF CADDY!*

I'LL DO BETTER NEXT TIME, SIR.

THERE WON'T *BE* A NEXT TIME! I'M THROUGH WITH GOLF! AS MY DEAR OLD FATHER USED TO SAY, "IF YOU CAN'T BEAT 'EM, THEN QUIT IN A *PETULANT HUFF!*"

NOW FIND SOMETHING ELSE FOR ME TO DO ON SUNDAY AFTERNOONS!

YES, SIR.

THE NEXT WEEK...

IF I MISS THIS SHOT, YOU *WIN AGAIN*, SIR.

YES! YES! JUST GET ON WITH IT!

DARN.

GOOD HEAVENS, SMITHERS! A LITTLE MORE *WILT* CHAMBERLAIN AND A LITTLE LESS *NEVILLE* CHAMBERLAIN!

PERHAPS WE SHOULD TRY A SPORT MORE SUITED TO YOUR *AGGRESSIVE NATURE,* SIR.

THE WEEK AFTER...

WELL DONE, SMITHERS! LOOK AT ME! COACH OF A PRO HOCKEY TEAM!

I THOUGHT YOU'D LIKE IT, SIR.

LIKE IT? I'M LIKE A KID IN A CANDY STORE!

BHAGAVAD GITA
3:16

YOU THERE. GO *SLASH* THAT OTHER FELLOW ON THE ANKLE. AND DON'T *SPARE THE LUMBER!*

DUFF BEER

LATER...

SWEET MARTY MCSORELY! NEXT TIME I WANT TO HIRE A BAND OF *BRUTAL THUGS* TO DO MY BIDDING, I'LL *BUY* AN ARMY OF *THIRD-WORLD MERCENARIES!* IT WOULD BE CHEAPER, AND *THEY* COME WITH GUNS!

PAYROLL

C.M. BURNS OWNER

"WHAT'S THIS THEN?"

IT'S CALLED *VIRTUAL REALITY*, SIR. I'VE HAD THE PROFESSOR DESIGN SOME *SCENARIOS* THAT I THOUGHT *YOU* MIGHT FIND APPEALING.

THAT'S THE "PILLAGING WITH GHENGIS KHAN" PROGRAM THAT YOU SEE NOW ЭNG-HEYЄ WITH THE LANCING AND THE SLAUGHTERING OF INNOCENTS AND SO FORTH.

HA, HA! SUPPLICATE BEFORE ME, ALL OF CHRISTENDOM!

WHY DON'T YOU TRY ANOTHER ONE, SIR?

HOW ABOUT "FIDDLING WITH NERO"?

OR "ENDANGERED-WHALE HUNTER"?

BAAAH! IF I WANT TO HUNT *ENDANGERED SEA MAMMALS,* I'LL DO IT LIKE I'VE ALWAYS DONE IT!

OF COURSE, SIR. I'LL BOOK TWO TICKETS TO SEA WORLD!

C.M. BURNS

NO, NO! WHO AM I KIDDING? GOLF IS MY *TRUE LOVE.* THE EASY CHEATING, THE DECADENCE OF THE GOLF CART, SHAVING BALD HUNDREDS OF ACRES OF FOREST, AND DIVERTING MILLIONS OF GALLONS OF PRECIOUS WATER.

BUT WHAT ABOUT THE TEEN-AGERS, SIR?

AS MY DEAR OLD FATHER USED TO SAY, "IF YOU DON'T LIKE THE OTHER PEOPLE ON THE GOLF COURSE, HAVE THEM ALL *KILLED.*"

BUT, SIR...!

ALWAYS THE WET BLANKET, EH, SMITHERS? NEVER MIND, I'VE GOT A *BETTER PLAN.* I SAY IF YOU CAN'T BEAT 'EM, THEN *BUILD* YOUR *OWN GOLF COURSE* AND *MAKE* YOUR *OWN RULES.*

AN EXCELLENT IDEA, SIR. BUT WHERE?

WHY NOT....

A WEEK LATER...

THE PLANS FOR YOUR *DREAM GOLF COURSE* ARE COMING TOGETHER NICELY, SIR.

GOLF IS NEARLY AS *ADDICTIVE* AS TOBACCO OR MILLION-DOLLAR GAME SHOWS, SO FINDING ENOUGH PEOPLE WILLING TO EXPEND A *SHAMEFUL AMOUNT* OF TIME AND MONEY CHASING A LITTLE WHITE BALL AROUND WILL BE EASY.

THE ONLY POSSIBLE HITCH IS THAT THE SITE YOU SELECTED IS RIGHT IN THE MIDDLE OF THE SPRINGFIELD NATURAL PRESERVE. THE LOCAL ENVIRONMENTAL COMMUNITY IS SURE TO *KICK UP A FUSS*.

WE'VE ALREADY RECEIVED *STRONGLY WORDED LETTERS* FROM STING AND LEONARDO DICAPRIO.

IS THAT SO?

LET ME TELL YOU SOMETHING, SMITHERS. IF YOU CAN FIND A *PASTIME* THAT A MAN WILL NEGLECT HIS CHILDREN AND FORSAKE HIS GOD TO ENJOY, *THAT'S* THE BUSINESS TO BE IN!

AND IF YOU HAPPEN TO *TORMENT* SOME SHAGGY-FACED GRADUATE STUDENTS AND SOME PRETTY BOY VAUDEVILLIANS ALONG THE WAY, WELL THAT'S JUST *GRAVY*!

... AND THOUGH *PLAYING* GOLF PROVIDES NO MORE EXERCISE THAN *WATCHING* GOLF ON TV, MILLIONS OF AMERICANS *STILL* CALL IT A SPORT. AND BECAUSE IT'S "BEER-FRIENDLY", IT'S A SPORT THAT MILLIONS OF AMERICANS *LOVE*.

YOU SAID IT, BROTHER.

SO, *HATS OFF* TO MONTGOMERY BURNS' PLANS FOR A NEW GOLF COURSE NESTLED IN THE HEART OF THE *SPRINGFIELD NATURAL PRESERVE*.

THAT'S *IMPOSSIBLE!* THAT FOREST IS *PROTECTED!*

PLANS FOR CUTTING 5000 ACRES OF 200-YEAR-OLD TREES FOR THE COURSE WERE GIVEN AN *ENTHUSIASTIC THUMBS-UP* BY THE *SPRINGFIELD ENVIRONMENTAL REVIEW BOARD*, WHICH, *COINCIDENTALLY...*

"...DISBANDED YESTERDAY AND *REFORMED* AS THE *SPRINGFIELD PORSCHE OWNERS CLUB*."

I'VE GOT TO *STOP* THIS! I'LL CALL AN *EMERGENCY MEETING* OF THE LI'L CHICKADEES!

HAVE YOU SEEN THIS, SMITHERS?

THE DEEP FRYER IN THE KITCHEN WILL BE HEATED BY BURNING THOSE *PESKY* 200-YEAR OLD TREES THOSE HIPPIES ARE FUSSING ABOUT.

SPEAKING OF THE ENVIRONMENTALISTS, SIR, A GROUP OF *MALCONTENTS*, CALLED THE LI'L CHICKADEES, IS ORGANIZING A *BLOCKADE* OF THE LOGGING ROAD.

LI'L CHICKADEES, EH? THEY SOUND LIKE A *VICIOUS BAND OF ANARCHISTS*. IT WILL GIVE ME GREAT PLEASURE TO "*CLIP THEIR WINGS*".

ACTUALLY, THEY'RE AN ORGANIZATION THAT TEACHES *OUTDOORSMANSHIP* AND *LEADERSHIP* TO CHILDREN.

CHILDREN? THEN IT WILL GIVE ME GREAT PLEASURE TO CLIP THEIR *TINY* WINGS! BWA-HA-HA!!!!

AT THE ENTRANCE TO THE SPRINGFIELD PRESERVE...

OAKS NOT STROKES!

TREES NOT TEES!

WOODS NOT WOODS!

LOOK AT THAT UNSIGHTLY GATHERING OF GREEN-PEACENIKS AND TROTSKYITES, SMITHERS. NOTHING GETS MY COCKLES UP LIKE THE FOUL STENCH OF ACTIVISM.

SHALL I RAM THEM AS USUAL, SIR?

NO. NOT TODAY.

THAT'S QUITE A *CHANGE OF HEART*, SIR!

WELL, IF *YOU* HAVE TO SPEND THE WHOLE MORNING WIPING HIPPIES OFF THE BUMPER, THEN *WHO* WILL HELP ME PLOT DIABOLICAL NEW WAYS OF MAKING MONEY? CERTAINLY NOT THAT FELLOW FROM THE TEMP AGENCY, I CAN TELL YOU THAT.

...CONVINCE POPULACE TO PAY $4.00 FOR BOTTLES OF WATER.

NO, CALL ME OLD-FASHIONED, BUT FOR BREAKING UP A DEMONSTRATION, NOTHING BEATS A PACK OF *RAVENOUS ATTACK DOGS!*

143

THIS WILL GIVE ME GREAT PLEASURE...

HMM...WHAT'S THIS? THE UNIFORM LOOKS STRANGELY FAMILIAR...

ⵑGASP!ⵑ

CHICKADEE TROOP 247

SHALL I RELEASE THE HOUNDS, SIR?

NO! STOP! AND TURN THIS CONVOY AROUND. WE'RE RETREATING!

GROOVY!

YAY!

FAR OUT!

DUUUDE!

WHAT'S WRONG, SIR? THE DOGS WERE *HUNGRY*, THAT MOTLEY CREW CLEARLY DESERVED A *SOUND MAULING*, AND THERE WERE *NO WITNESSES*. WHY DID YOU *RELENT*?

BECAUSE OF AN *OATH* I SWORE MANY YEARS AGO.

AN OATH, SIR? I'LL TALK TO OUR *LEGAL DEPARTMENT*. AS YOU KNOW, THEY CAN FIND A WAY FOR YOU TO *WEASEL OUT* OF ANY PROMISE YOU MAY HAVE MADE.

NO, THIS IS ONE OATH I WON'T BE WEASLING OUT OF, FOR YOU SEE...

...I AM A CHICKADEE!

A CHICKADEE?

WELL, WHEN I WAS A MEMBER WE WERE CALLED *THE LEGION OF THE HOODED FALCON*. THAT WAS BEFORE THE ACLU AND THOSE PINKO GAL GROUPS STARTED RUNNING THE COUNTRY. I DIDN'T MAKE THE CONNECTION UNTIL I SAW *THE UNIFORM* ON THAT YOUNG GIRL.

"THE LEGION OF THE HOODED FALCON?" I HAD NO IDEA, SIR.

THOSE WERE HAPPY TIMES. DAYS FILLED WITH RUNNING, CLIMBING, KILLING, AND SKINNING.

NIGHTS OF CAMP-OUTS, SING-A-LONGS, AND, OF COURSE, *MORE* KILLING AND SKINNING.

I EVEN KEPT MY OLD UNIFORM. SO MANY MEMORIES...

THIS ONE IS FOR MAKING AN *ICE BUCKET* FROM A *RHINO HOOF*. IT'S NOT AS EASY AS IT SOUNDS.

VIVISECTION

GENTLEMEN'S FURNISHINGS

SEIGE

WHAT ABOUT THE OATH, SIR?

YOU SEE, SMITHERS, IF I HAD RELEASED THE HOUNDS, I WOULD HAVE BROKEN *THE CHICKADEE CODE*.

THE CHICKADEE CODE?

"THOUGH TORMENTED BY BEASTS AND BIRDS, AND EVIL FISHES OF THE STREAM, THE VICTOR OF THE NIGHT OF TERROR SHALL BE...."

"...THE ONE THAT DOES NOT SCREAM!"

COOL!

THAT NIGHT...

THANKS FOR COMING INTO THE WOODS WITH ME FOR THE "NIGHT OF TERROR", BART.

SURE THING, LISA.

I FIGURE THAT A WORLD CLASS PRANKSTER LIKE YOU WILL BE ABLE TO SEE THROUGH ANY TRICKS THAT MR. BURNS MIGHT TRY AND PULL....

...AND YOU MIGHT JUST HAVE A FEW PRANKS OF YOUR OWN UP YOUR SLEEVE.

ITS ALL HERE, LISA. RUBBER SPIDER. RUBBER SNAKE...

...REAL SNAKE...

SSSSSSS!

ARE YOU SURE YOU WANT TO DO THIS, SIR? THEY ARE, AFTER ALL, JUST CHILDREN.

WELL THEN, WHO ENJOYS A "PRANK" MORE THAN "JUST CHILDREN?"

NOW RELEASE THIS HIDEOUS SNAKE NEAR THEIR TENT!

THIS IS POSITIVELY...

...DESPICABLE!

151

"...IT'S *SURE* TO BE SCARING THOSE CHILDREN JUST AS MUCH AS US."

ZZZZZ...

ZZZZZ...

AHHHHHHHHHH!

VRRREEEOOOOOOOO

DID YOU HEAR THAT? IT WAS A *SCREAM!*

I HEARD LOTS OF SCREAMS. I'VE BEEN LISTENING TO THIS *DEATH METAL* TAPE THAT OTTO MADE FOR ME.

IT'S STOPPED, SIR.

YOU SCREAMED! WE *WIN!* THE FOREST IS *SAVED!*

ALL RIGHT! YOU AND YOUR TREE-HUGGING, BUSH-LOVING FRIENDS CAN HAVE YOUR BLESSED PRESERVE! I JUST WANT TO KNOW ONE THING: HOW COULD A PAIR OF *PINK-CHEEKED MOPPETS* MAKE SUCH *BLOOD CHILLING NOISES?*

AS MUCH AS WE'D LIKE TO TAKE CREDIT, IT WASN'T US.

THEN WHO?

ARE YOU *LADIES* ALL RIGHT?

OH! MR. BURNS. WE HEARD *GIRLISH* SCREAMS.

LOGGERS!

WE WERE JUST GEARING UP TO START CUTTING.

YOU WERE MAKING THOSE HORRIBLE NOISES?!

YOU WERE GOING TO CUT DOWN THE FOREST ANYWAY? YOU WERE GOING TO CHEAT! WHAT ABOUT THE CODE OF THE CHICKADEES?

WHAT CAN I SAY? OLD HABITS DIE HARD. COME ON, SMITHERS.

SIR, ARE YOU SURE YOU DON'T WANT TO HAVE ANOTHER GO AT BUILDING YOUR DREAM GOLF COURSE? OUR LEGAL DEPARTMENT HAS FOUND A *LOOP HOLE* IN THE CHICKADEE CODE.

NO, SMITHERS, I THINK I'VE FOUND MY "DREAM GOLF COURSE".

I'VE HAD THE PROFESSOR HERE ADJUST THIS VIDEO MACHINE IN A MANNER THAT IS *MOST PLEASING*!

FORE!

ZZAP!

"NOW *THIS* IS GOLFING!"

THE END

HEY! HAVE YOU NOTICED THAT GOLF IS HARDLY EVER AS EXCITING AS IT WAS IN "CADDYSHACK" OR "HAPPY GILMORE"?

NOW THINGS WOULD BE DIFFERENT...

...IF HOMER SIMPSON INVENTED GOLF!

IAN BOOTHBY
WRITER

PHIL ORTIZ
PENCILS

JASON HO
MIKE ROTE
BILL MORRISON
INKS

KAREN BATES
LETTERS

ART VILLANUEVA
COLORS

"*REGULAR HOLES* WOULD BE REPLACED BY *DONUT HOLES!*"

MMMMM... PAR 4.

"GOLF COURSES WOULD BE LESS *SNOOTY* ABOUT THEIR *DRESS CODES*."

UH...I'M AFRAID YOU'RE *A-FRAYED* IN THE *CABOOSE* THERE, HOMER.

NOW *THERE'S* A HOLE IN ONE I DIDN'T NEED TO SEE!!

"BORING GOLF CARTS WOULD BE REPLACED BY *THE BATMOBILE*, *GENERAL LEE* AND *KITT* FROM 'KNIGHT RIDER'!"

MICHAEL, YOU'RE SLICING TO THE LEFT.

SHUT UP, KITT!

"THERE WOULD BE LESS *WAITING AROUND*..."

"...AND MORE *BODY-CHECKING!*"

GAAAAA-DIDDLY-AAAAH!

"LESS *POLITE GOLF*

SMATTER! SMATTER! SMATTER!

"...AND MORE *EXTREME GOLF DANCERS!*"

Everybody putt now!

"*WATER TRAPS* WOULD BE REPLACED WITH *BEER TRAPS!*"

MY BALL WENT IN. I GUESS THAT'S A STROKE...

I'LL GET IT!

"*SAND TRAPS* WOULD BE MORE *TRAPPY!*"

THROW ME THE CLUB! THROW ME THE CLUB!

"*GRASS* WOULD BE REPLACED BY THAT RUBBER THEY MAKE *SUPER BALLS* WITH!"

BOING!

BOING!

BOING!

"*GOLF LINKS* WOULD BE REPLACED BY..."

"...*PORK LINKS!*"

"ALL MATH WOULD BE *GONE!*"

I SHOT A *5* ON THAT HOLE, AND YOU SHOT A 12.

SO WE'RE TIED.

BUT I...WELL, THERE'S ANOTHER SCHOOL SUBJECT THAT HAS NO USE IN THE REAL WORLD.

"AND THERE'D BE MORE **WINDMILLS**, **GORILLAS** AND **FLYING SAUCERS!** WHY SHOULD MINIATURE GOLF COURSES GET ALL THE GOOD STUFF?"

"NO MORE **EARLY TEE TIMES**, UNLESS YOU CAN PLAY FROM **BED!**"

GOOD SHOT MR...**UGH** SIMPSON!

¿YAWN!¿ WAKE ME WHEN WE GET TO THE GREEN!

¿GRUNT!¿

WHACK!

"THINGS WOULD **HAVE LESS EMBARRASSING NAMES!**"

I THINK I BENT MY **SHAFT** AGAIN.

YOU NEED TO CHANGE YOUR GRIP AND QUIT **WHACKING** SO HARD.

AT LEAST I GOT A **BOGEY**, AND EVERYONE SAW IT.

NOW IF YOU'LL EXCUSE ME, I'M GONNA USE THE **BALL WASHER**.

"**TAG TEAMS** WOULD BE **LEGAL!**"

FINISH THIS OFF FOR ME, WILL YA, TIGER?

BUT...BUT...

SURE THING, HOMER!

SMAK!

WOODS

"WE'D HAVE LESS GOVERNMENT REGULATION OF **SURFACE TO AIR MISSILE LAUNCHERS**..."

BOOM!

...AND THERE SHOULD BE MORE **ROBOTS** WITH **DOG CADDIES** AND ANOTHER THING...

HE'S BEEN LIKE THIS FOR AN HOUR.

WHY DO YOU EVEN **HAVE** A PLACE LIKE THIS ON A GOLF COURSE? I DON'T UNDERSTAND THIS GAME AT ALL.

NOW IF **MARGE SIMPSON** INVENTED GOLF...

THE END